WITCHCRAFT

 a beginner's guide

TERESA MOOREY

Headway · Hodder & Stoughton

Acknowledgements

Thanks to Shan, from the House of the Goddess, to Daniel Cohen of *Wood & Water* magazine, to Phillip Day of Pan Pacific Pagan Alliance, the Pagan Federation, and Sean Knight, Secretary of the National Management Council of the Church of All Worlds in Australia for providing helpful information for this book. Illustrations by Dark Moon Designs, Tel: 01273 623321.

Orders: please contact Bookpoint Ltd, 39 Milton Park, Abingdon, Oxon OX14 4TD. Telephone: (44) 01235 400414, Fax: (44) 01235 400454. Lines are open from 9.00–6.00, Monday to Saturday, with a 24 hour message answering service. Email address: orders@bookpoint.co.uk

British Library Cataloguing in Publication Data

Vidgen-Moorey, Teresa
Witchcraft: a beginner's guide
1.Witchcraft
1.Title
133.4'3

ISBN 0 340 670142

First published 1996

Impression number	15	14	13	12	11	10	9	8	7	6	
Year		2004	2003	2002	2001	2000	1999	1998			

Typeset by Transet Limited, Coventry, England.
Printed in Great Britain for Hodder & Stoughton Educational, a division of Hodder Headline Plc, 338 Euston Road, London NW1 3BH by Cox & Wyman Ltd, Reading.

OTHER TITLES IN THIS SERIES

Chakras 0 340 62082 X   How to work with chakras, the body's energy centres, in safety and with confidence.

Chinese Horoscopes 0 340 64804 X   How to determine your own Chinese horoscope, what personality traits you are likely to have, and how your fortunes may fluctuate in years to come.

Dowsing 0 340 60882 X   How to start dowsing – what to use, what to dowse, and what to expect when subtle energies are detected.

Dream Interpretation 0 340 601150 7   How to unravel the meaning behind dream images to interpret your own and other people's dreams.

Feng Shui 0 340 62079 X   How to increase your good fortune and well-being by harmonising your environment with the natural energies of the earth.

Gems and Crystals 0 340 60883 8   All you need to know about choosing, keeping and using stones to increase your personal awareness and improve your well-being.

Graphology 0 340 60625 8   How to make a comprehensive analysis of your own and other people's handwriting to reveal the hidden self.

I Ching 0 340 62080 3   An introduction to the ancient beauty of the *I Ching* or *Book of Changes* – its history, survival and modern day applications.

Love Signs 0 340 64805 8   The important roles played by each of the planets, focusing particularly on the position of the Moon at the time of birth.

Meditation 0 340 64835 X   How to start meditating and benefiting from this ancient mental discipline immediately. Highly illustrated and full colour.

Numerology 0 340 59551 5   All the information you will need to understand the significance of numbers in your everyday life.

Palmistry 0 340 59552 3   What to look for and how to interpret what you find, using the oldest form of character reading still in use.

Runes 0 340 62081 1   How runes can be used in our technological age to increase personal awareness and stimulate individual growth.

Star Signs 0 340 59553 1   How your star sign affects everything about you. How to use this knowledge in your relationships and in everyday life.

Tarot 0 340 59550 7   Which cards to buy, where to get them and how to use them as a tool for gaining self-knowledge, while exploring present and future possibilities. Full colour.

The Moon and You 0 340 64836 8   Analysis of the nine Lunar Types. How to find your moon phase and how to tune into it.

Visualisation 0 340 65495 3   How to practise the basic techniques – to relieve stress, improve your health and increase your sense of personal well-being.

To all those who have gone before.
'May we meet know and remember, and love them again'.

CONTENTS

INTRODUCTION

*... deep questions... are meant not to generate dogma
but to propel us on journeys*
                    Starhawk, *The Spiral Dance*

L ots of things in this book have been quite difficult to put into
words. Something gets lost or changed along the way. Like trying
to catch mist, you can only do it by condensing it, and then it has
turned into droplets of water. Nor Hall says:

> Experience that cannot be articulated is generally undervalued
> in a world ignorant of the mysteries. Such a world creates
> psychic havoc for people whose mode of existence is
> feminine... they haven't any words to convey the essence of
> primary experience.   *(The Moon and the Virgin)*

Nor Hall is speaking about such things as motherhood and tending
the dying, but the words are equally valid for witchcraft, for it partakes
of 'the mysteries' and is often worse than 'undervalued'.

This book is for people who are attracted to witchcraft but are
unsure of what it involves. These are the 'beginners' – but no witch
is truly a beginner, for witchcraft comes from within. However, one
has to start somewhere! This is not a step-by-step manual, but if
you thumb through it, you can construct your approach. If your
approach is serious you may find some of the questions flippant, so
pass those quickly. If you are an intrigued sceptic, or have just
wondered about tall hats and broomsticks this book is also for you.
I've tried to be as clear as possible to dispel misconceptions.
Witches don't seek conversions – but acceptance would be nice!

Let me also stress that none of this is the last word on anything. Every witch is unique. Books 'for beginners' usually put across a basic set of rules or method of approach, but I want my approach to be different. The traditions are there, but my views creep in. So take what feels good, and leave what doesn't. Besides, as witchcraft becomes more open it is growing, changing and adapting, cross-fertilising with psychotherapy and politics, and generally preparing to blossom in the twenty-first century.

I hope this book can help the process. If you are interested please don't stop here. There is a list of further reading at the back. *Paganism for Beginners* is a companion volume in this series, describing Wicca and other forms of paganism more fully. Take time to develop your own thoughts – they are important.

Blessed be in the Goddess.

THE SACRED ART

Oh, I have been and I have seen
In magic worlds of Otherwhere
For all this world may praise or blame
For ban or blessing nought I care

Doreen Valiente, *The Witch's Ballad*

What is a witch?

Witches are great individualists, so there are probably as many different answers to this as there are witches!

A witch is a person who perceives vividly the connection between all aspects of life. Witches do not see spirit and matter as separate

entities – they worship Nature in stream and stone, plants, animals and people. They usually have a well-developed instinctual side. Also witches are vibrantly aware of unseen natural energies – which they use in their spellworkings. Herbs, colours, symbols – all these have properties that witches make use of, mostly to help and heal.

Most witches have more than a trace of mysticism which they develop by trancework, but they are also great pragmatists who value common sense and Mother wit – for, as you will see, witchcraft is a sensible matter, for the most part. Often deeply sensitive, they feel for each felled tree and wounded animal, but they are also tough. They accept that death is part of life and that suffering has a purpose.

Needless to say, witches are not the frightening hags of children's stories! They don't wear tall hats or ride on broomsticks. The idea about the hats may have come from the 'cone of power' that witches raise, and the broomstick is a symbol of fertility – we shall be looking at these later on. Nor do witches blight cattle or have dealings with the devil. These ideas are the product of medieval imagination and came in handy for anyone corrupt who needed scapegoats! The ideas are hard to refute, and most people who don't know a real witch have their doubts. But such fears can bar the way to valuable knowledge. Witches have a saying: 'where there's fear there's power'.

What do witches believe in?

Believe 'in' is a funny idea to a witch. They don't perform acts of faith or have dogmas. To a witch the Goddess and the God are just there, like the hills and rivers are there. The Earth is the body of the Goddess. The God is the life force that impregnates. Goddess and God are within each of us. There is no idea of a separate God in heaven, judging us, nor the slightest belief that our bodies and their needs and pleasures are dirty or sinful, needing to be risen above to find salvation. The Goddess and God are sometimes called 'the Old Ones' for They have been with us since Neolithic times.

Some people are surprised to find that witchcraft is a religion, but really you can't be aware of spiritual realms and not be religious.

4

The witches' religion is free and unstructured, with no dogma. This can be something of a culture shock when dogma and religion have been seen as inseparable for so many hundreds of years! Above all to witches, life and the forces of Nature are sacred – there to be respected, celebrated and also used, when the time is right, in magical workings. Witches do not believe that their way is the one and only right way for everyone – they merely feel it is right for them. They believe strongly that each person should have the freedom to find his or her own way of worship, or not worshipping, as the case may be.

Why do witches have a Goddess and a God?

As we shall see, witches regard sexuality as sacred and the male/female polarity is a source of power. Thus it is only fitting that both should be seen as divine.

It seems pointless to assert that men and women are equal when God is continually referred to as 'He' – a little pronoun like that resonates deep in the unconscious, and despite all rationalisation results in a basic concept of God as masculine. Likewise myths are the dramatic representation of beliefs and where these are without the Goddess, the power of the Feminine cannot emerge. Witches believe that the Feminine is resoundingly important, and the reasons for many of the environmental problems that bedevil us have their roots in the underlying contempt for the Feminine over the last 2000 years (at least!). The Earth is the body of the Goddess. If you venerate Her you do not pollute Her – quite simple. That is a matter of instinct, not a law that needs to be imposed from without, or a matter of scientific proof.

If we wish to be philosophically correct, some see the Goddess and the God as emanating from an ineffable One – by definition unknowable. This is sometimes referred to as Ain Soph, a Qabalistic term – the Qabala is an ancient mystical doctrine. The more pragmatic feel this is irrelevant – it all depends on your point of view.

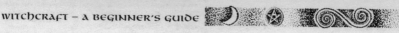

Do witches have a moral code?

Yes, and this is it.

> *Eight words the witches' creed fulfil.*
> *If it harms none, do what you will.*

Witches believe in freedom and personal choice. They also believe in responsibility. You have to decide yourself what 'harms none', but mostly this is quite obvious. Stealing, bullying, assault – these are obviously harmful. Occasionally issues are less clear, however. In a divorce, for instance, people may be harmed, but equally they may be harmed if the marriage remains intact. There is no dogma to tell you what you must and must not do. 'Harming none' also means not harming yourself. There is no law that says you must put yourself last and go through life a po-faced martyr (probably poisoning the air for everyone that somes near). We are each responsible for our own fulfilment and happiness, for only in this way can we truly celebrate life and be creative – and only in this way can we bring anything worth having into our relationships with other people. So although the witches' code is simple in one way, in another it is also complicated. 'Do what you will' is not an invitation to rampant self-indulgence! It needs thought about what is really right for you, your 'true will' not just the whims of the ego.

Do witches believe in reincarnation?

Many witches do believe that we are born again. After all, life ebbs and flows in cycles, winter is followed by spring, night is followed by day, and it seems reasonable that the same should be true of human life. Besides, working magic brings with it a consciousness of other levels of existence beyond the physical, to which it seems a human soul might retreat in between lives. Memories of former lives are common among witches, and this may be because the lives of witches are in some ways more vivid (and, until recently, more dangerous) because witchcraft is practised in succeeding lives. It is said 'Once a witch, always a witch' and that doesn't necessarily

mean only one lifespan! There is so much to learn and experience, so much growth possible, that to restrict it to one life does seem rather meaningless. However, whether the belief in reincarnation is literal or not, in general witches see death as a transformation, rather than an end, for energy is never destroyed, only transmuted.

ARE WITCHES THE SAME AS BLACK MAGICIANS AND SATANISTS?

The answer is a definite 'no'. The reason for this is simple. Satan, or the devil is a Christian concept. He is seen as acting against God, tempting mortals into sin and damnation – a force of evil. Witches do not believe in such a force, and so they cannot possibly be Satanists. You need to believe in the concept of Christianity to worship the devil. Of course, some fanatics will accuse witches of worshipping the devil anyway, because they see anything that does not fit in with their view of religion as evil. It seems there were plenty of such people about in the Middle Ages. However, witches see both darkness and light, creation and destruction as part of the Goddess and the God. They do not split anything off and call it forbidden and unmentionable. The devil has been used as a dumping ground for all that is unpleasant and repressed – as have witches themselves. There certainly is evil, and a look back through history reveals that the most horrible cruelty and destruction have been carried out by the very people who set themselves up to destroy 'evil' – witch-hunters, inquisitors, Nazis. This sort of thing is still going on today, in places.

The Black Magician issue needs to be resolved. In the first place, a magician is not quite the same as a witch. Traditionally witchcraft has been simple and natural. Sweeping the floor or brushing your hair can be turned into a spell by a resourceful witch. Witches came mainly from the poorer classes and were more often than not women – busy women, with children, animals and old people to look after. The magicians of old tended to be more well-off and influential. They were often men, and their magic involved more ceremony and planning. Of course, the approaches often merged and still do.

The 'black' question is an important matter. Magic is a force, like electricity, and can be directed by the practitioner. Unlike electricity, however, it is not quite so impersonal. There are certain occult laws, and to work magic you have to develop a magical consciousness. With this consciousness in place you are fully aware of the consequences to yourself of malevolent actions. Most witches would not attempt anything black – there really is little point. Spells are mostly joyful things that make you feel good, and you get the best results from positive means. Those who wish to harm – and there will always be the odd one – succeed mostly in harming themselves. The black magic stories that we hear from time to time are the product of paranoia, fevered imagination and sometimes some nasty messing about by people who enjoy being shocking.

WHEN WERE WITCHES PERSECUTED?

Throughout history all societies have been uneasy regarding people they saw as a threat to the State through the manipulation of subtle forces, but only relatively recently did almost anyone who moved in the realms of the hidden and instinctual run the risk of being considered evil, or potentially so. It was believed that the witches' powers would die only if their bodies were burnt.

In the 'Dark Ages' the Church sought to dispel pagan customs. In fact, they incorporated many of these into the Church calendar and many Christian saints are reappearances of old gods – St Bridget is a good example of this, having many of the attributes of the Irish goddess Bridget/Brighid/Bride. In the eighth century a Church document called the *Canon Episcopi* officially stated that witches were an illusion, but this was reversed by the Inquisition – an arm of the Church especially instituted to root out and extinguish heresy – and by the end of the fifteenth century it was considered to be heretical if one did not believe in witches. The main persecutions took place in the fifteenth, sixteenth and seventeenth centuries in Europe and the British Isles. In England officially it was illegal to torture suspects and they were hanged, not burnt. However, this was not the case in Scotland or the rest of Europe.

As the 'Age of Reason' was ushered in with the eighteenth century, interest in witches dwindled. In 1736 witchcraft ceased to be a capital charge in Scotland and England. The last documented witch-burning in the British Isles took place in Scotland in 1722, when Janet Horne was executed. However, treason involving witchcraft was still subject to this punishment, and for a woman to kill her husband was called 'petty treason'. As late as 1776 a woman was burned for this in Horsham, England. It is worthy of note that the same penalty was not inflicted upon men who killed their wives.

Why were witches persecuted?

This is a complex and important question, that is connected with the reasons why the word 'witch' makes people uneasy, even today. To understand persecution we need to digress a bit into the realms of psychology, because the roots are often in paranoia. Paranoia is usually understood as irrational fear, and indeed it is. People were afraid of witches. However, the basis of paranoia is a split in the personality, where bits of ourselves that we are unable to acknowledge get pushed into the unconscious. They don't stay there, however. By a mechanism called projection they seem to alight on people and things outside ourselves. So these things may acquire a power to terrify and enrage us out of all proportion to anything real.

Of course, it all feels very real to this type of paranoid, who sees the unpleasant elements as evil and outside oneself, and it gains in momentum when it is an idea that takes over a large group of people or a country. This concept is explored further by Norman Cohn in *Europe's Inner Demons* (Basic Books, New York, 1975). (In fact, he seems to think that witchcraft existed only in fantasy.) But however many Jews, witches or black people are victimised, the fear never goes away.

To a greater or lesser extent, most of us are a little paranoid. This can be hard to understand. As an example: we may heartily detest people who are the life and soul of parties. Deep inside we may truly yearn to be the centre of attention ourselves, but may have been told, as we were growing up that no-one would like us if we showed off. So

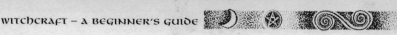

we are no longer even conscious of our desire to take centre stage – we just hate others who hog the limelight. This description of paranoia is not complete of course, for it is a complex condition. It is graphically explained in *Families and How to Survive Them* by Skynner and Cleese (Methuen, 1983).

The struggle to face up to such things, comparatively small though they may be, can be awful, undertaken in private moments, with shudders and feeling hot all over. So, horror of horrors – we are the very thing we detest. In the climate of acceptance and personal growth fostered today it is hard enough. Imagine what it was like hundreds of years ago, when the desire to direct one's life or enjoy sex were believed punishable by eternal damnation. Much easier to declare oneself humble and chaste and hunt down the 'witches' instead. Paranoia, sadism and greed (witches' goods were often confiscated by witchfinders) all empowered the tide of horror and cruelty that saw the murder of countless people in the Middle Ages. Some say as many as nine million – mostly women – lost their lives.

Although the above isn't really about witchcraft I think it is important to understand the reason why people still fear the word 'witch' today. But the word needs to be vindicated, because so many people have died in its name. Other reasons for the persecution may have been because 'witches' made handy scapegoats, and also because the gods of the old religion became the devils of the new. The witches' Horned God became the devil. This seems to have been an attempt to get control over the followers of the old ways and to convince everyone that forms of paganism such as witchcraft were evil.

In 1951 the laws against witchcraft were repealed, in England. Today witches in many countries are more fortunate – we are free to explore and develop.

Tell me more about the Goddess

The Goddess is the substance of the Universe. She is the womb from which we, and all of life have sprung. In *Man and His Symbols*, C G Jung says '... we talk of matter... We conduct laboratory experiments...

But the word 'matter' remains a dry... intellectual concept... How different was the former image of matter – the Great Mother – that could... express the... emotional meaning of Mother Earth.' Jung realised that the devaluation of the Feminine held great significance in human history and for our mental and spiritual state. However, witches have always honoured the Great Feminine in Her myriad forms.

The Goddess is all around us as Mother Earth, Moon and stars. She is there in each clod and bush and the air we breathe. She is us, for our bodies are part of Her, yet She is still a mystery, for we can never know Her totally. In *The Charge* (an ancient Goddess invocation reconstructed by Doreen Valiente), She says 'Behold, all acts of love and pleasure are my rituals'. We approach the Goddess not through self-denial, but through enjoyment of Her gifts, not the least of which is sexual love. By identifying with our bodies we partake of Her. This may seem surprising after centuries of teaching that the spirit can be approached only by overcoming the body. What a cruel and distorting message!

Fang, claw and winter wind are the Goddess too, for She also brings the destruction that is necessary for the continuance of life. Any creative act requires some demolition. For instance, making a garden means killing weeds and slugs. So the Goddess is death as well as life.

In many ways femaleness precedes maleness, for the foetus is female at first and masculine characteristics overlay this later for a male child. In evolution the female seems to have come before the male. There is strong evidence that worship of a Great Mother predated worship of a God by thousands of years. In the *Vangelo* of the witches of Tuscany (translated by Charles Leland) we are told 'Diana was the first created before all creation; in her were all things; out of herself, the first darkness, she divided herself...'. There are many, many stories in many different cultures that tell how the primordial Goddess gave birth to all the other gods. She also gives birth to Her own consort, the son/lover – but more of this later. So to witches the Goddess is first. That doesn't mean superior, for witchcraft is about balance, but it does mean we give our Mother proper respect. In human families, respect for mother, return to the family home, the caring, sharing and communicating this gives rise to, is the basis for our culture.

As celestial feminine the Goddess is also the Moon, our nearest neighbour in space, ruler of the tides and the ebb and flow of the life force. The Moon is cyclical, like women who have a menstrual cycle. Besides this, the three phases of the Moon correspond to the three stages in a woman's life – maiden, mother and crone. From this comes the idea of the Triple Goddess, expressing each special phase of femininity.

The waxing Moon is the Maiden – adventurous, full of initiative, ideas, freshness. The Full Moon is the time of the Mother, representing fulfilment, culmination, bounty, but also balance. The Mother also brings knowledge of things that won't work and have to be abandoned. The waning Moon is the time of the Crone, bringer of wisdom, guardian of secrets – sometimes Goddess of Death. The concept of a Triple Goddess was pervasive, many goddesses having three forms. At any time in her life a woman can find within her the energies and qualities of any of the three. Witches usually regard the phases of the Moon as important in spellwork, and most spells are best carried out when the Moon is waxing, or at the powerful time when she is Full.

Each woman embodies the Goddess, each man carries Her within him as his 'inner feminine' helping him to relate to women and to find his own sensitivity. The Goddess can teach true respect for the gifts of the body, as opposed to exploiting it, and the material world which in a sense is the body of the Goddess – the words 'matter' and 'mother' come from the same root. We don't have to look far to see that this respect has been conspicuously lacking. From nuclear warheads to credit cards our culture is full of signs that we have departed miles from a proper appreciation of the material, as opposed to an obsession with conquering and possessing it. Our Goddess can show us the way back to something more sensible – a true love for and enjoyment of Nature. As witches we work continuously to see Her re-enshrined. Many of us believe that Her banishment is closely linked to the damage that has been done to the ecosystem. We can also see that most wars are a result of one dogmatic, patriarchal philosophy trying to stamp out another. The Goddess is not a panacea, but She is badly needed as a balancing force.

Tell me more about the God

The God is the life force, the impregnator. He initiates change and action. He is movement and purpose. His force surges with each brave spring bloom, each sticky bud. He empowers and protects the creations of the Goddess. As Lord of the Dance He embodies wild delight, and as The Hunter He expresses the raw urge to survive, but He takes only that which is necessary. He suffers with His prey – in a way He also **is** the prey – for it is an esoteric truth that predator and prey are linked, and we should always respect that which gives us life. (It is said that 'you are what you eat'. So if what we eat has been over-hunted, over-farmed, reared in abominable conditions and treated with callous cruelty, what does that say about us?)

Shown as the Horned God, He is phallic and fierce. The horns depict the crescent moons, the sweeping fallopian tubes of a woman's reproductive system, or simply animal exuberance. Our concept of the God also embodies logic, but the God of the Witches tends to be more playful and instinctual, for this has been neglected. Once more to quote C G Jung '... what was the spirit is now identified with intellect and thus ceases to be the Father of All. It has degenerated to the limited ego-thoughts of man; the immense emotional energy expressed by the image of 'our Father' vanishes into the sand of an intellectual desert.' (Man and His Symbols).

I think it is much harder to arrive at an inspiring portrait of the God, than it is the Goddess, for She has been guarded. Repressed, denied and demeaned, women have been in a sense free to retreat. As long as they kept quiet they had a chance of being left in peace, and either consciously, but mostly instinctively, continued to cherish the Goddess in their talents and accomplishments, even though these were criminally devalued. Now She is re-emerging, sometimes savagely angry as warrior goddess, but mostly, it seems, delightfully intact.

I am not saying no distortion has taken place, because of course it has. Anything forced underground cannot thrive. However, for men, masculinity and the God, the perversion has in a sense been more grievous, simply because 'God' was so clearly defined as law-giver

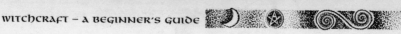

and punisher. The rediscovery of the warm and mirthful witches' God is part of a new awakening, and we badly need this protective model.

We have seen how many mythologies describe the Great Mother giving birth to a son, who becomes Her lover, impregnates Her and Dies, to be reborn again as Her son – and so the cycle continues. We shall be looking at the 'love story' of the Goddess and God and how this parallels the cycles of nature when we look at the Sabbats in Chapter 7. It must also be said that although the Goddess mates with Her son, witches do not believe in incest! This is all symbolic, and when the God mates with the Goddess He has left behind all identity as Her son. He is Her equal in age and experience as They resume the dance of love.

The God as son/lover is dual, being both the created and the creator. Also the God is seen as the Sun which 'dies' each year, and then 'resurrects' as spring approaches. Many mythologies celebrate the death and rebirth of a solar hero or Sun God, and kings were sometimes willing sacrifices in honour of this process. Besides, when a man makes love he is spent, giving up vitality with his seed. Of course, he soon recovers to mate again, but for a woman love-making is generally more diffuse and if she wishes she may simply continue. The Sun impregnates the land, and is spent, to rise again to impregnate once more next spring. The land itself, as Goddess, remains constantly with us, although altering Her aspect. Ancient people sometimes represented the mating of God and Goddess by constructing long barrows whose depths were penetrated by the rays of the Sun on certain dates – a vivid and touching metaphor.

As Lord of Light the God represents all that is vital. As Lord of Death He is the wise comforter and master of secret lore. Of course, none of us is purely masculine or feminine – each of us can consciously partake of Goddess or God, although for most women the Goddess will be the more accessible, while for the majority of men the same can be said for the God. The God can awaken in a woman her ability to protect herself and her creativity, to assert herself, to leave her inhibitions and find unbridled joy in the whirl of life.

My definitions are not stereotypes. Masculinity and femininity are most subtle – the more you try to define them the more differences seem to disappear, and yet polarity exists. Creative polarity also

exists between listener and symphony, observer and masterpiece. It is also there in homosexual relationships. Please don't take my descriptions as any sort of last word. They are my ideas at present and I believe generally representative, but they are not cast in marble.

We need both our Goddess and our God. They are the divine partnership of creation. As witches we work our magic to bring about true respect for the Earth and a reconciliation of opposites. A dream? Yes, but if you don't have a dream then how can you have a dream come true?

WHY ARE THERE LOTS OF DIFFERENT GODDESSES AND GODS?

Creation is so varied that no one goddess or god can express all at once – at least not graphically, or with a delicate and personal touch. Witches are pagans, and so see divinity everywhere. One goddess will best express our feelings about spring. Another will seem to embody the implacability of tempest. One god may represent all that is phallic, another may represent wisdom. More complex, each tree, stone and river can be seen as possessing its own spirit-god. Even our homes have gods, upon the threshold, the hearth, our beds. To be pedantic we can say these are all faces of one Goddess and God, but witchcraft is about the heart and this is better served by a colourful array of deities. *Paganism for Beginners* gives some examples of specific deities.

Later in the text some individual names of gods and goddesses will appear. The simplest way to understand this is that some witches think there is one Goddess and God, as described earlier in this chapter, others think in terms of many different gods and goddesses, and they take names and identities from any ancient pantheon that appeals: Celtic, Greek/Roman, Egyptian – whatever. This is colourful and inspiring. More confusing if you are new to these ideas can be the fact that a witch may at one time think in terms of one Goddess and God and at another in terms of many different goddesses and gods – I'm of that group. It must also be said that certain witches

are primarily concerned with the Goddess, and only marginally, if at all with the God. Possibly some are concerned mostly with the God. The point is that to a witch, as to most pagans, the gods are concepts with which to conjure and create, not rigid entities. There is a consistency of 'feeling' behind all this, but it is not anything like the familiar crystallised structures of dogma.

Do witches get together in covens?

Yes, they do. Witches who usually work alone may meet for a special purpose or for a festival. However, the term 'coven' generally applies to a group who regularly work together, under a High Priestess and High Priest. This type of witchcraft is more usually called 'Wicca', although there are less formal groupings and these seem to be gaining in popularity. Covens can really be of any practical number from three upwards. They do not have to consist of thirteen, as sometimes believed. Thirteen is a number special to witches, as the Moon makes thirteen circuits of the Zodiac in a year – and lunar instinctual knowledge is what witchcraft is all about. Some traditions state that thirteen should be the maximum number of persons in a coven, after which they should divide, so spreading the Craft. The Craft is a term for Wicca, and also witchcraft.

In medieval times the integrity of the coven was a matter of life and death. One person, sometimes called the 'man in black' would take messages between covens. People would know only the members of their immediate coven, so they could not betray others. However, it must be stated that much historical information is quite inaccurate, as it was extracted under torture from people who were, for the most part, certainly not witches by any definition.

What is Wicca?

Wicca can be termed 'group witchcraft' but that is rather an oversimplification. There are other types of groups with a looser structure, a more open style, and often with community involvements,

such as public festivals and courses. Wicca in its present form has been around since the 1940s. It is more regimented although the underlying beliefs are very similar. Wiccans form covens and call themselves 'witches'. They celebrate the eight seasonal festivals or 'Sabbats' and have a hierarchy of initiations. Wicca is both a religion and magical system. If working efficiently it can also be a means to self-development (as indeed can other paths). Wicca is discussed in *Paganism – a beginner's guide*.

bow is Wicca different from Lone witchcraft?

In Wicca there is the comfort and support of a group and also the possibility of a good party! The High Priestess and High Priest are there to teach beginners about the Craft and rituals are prescribed and sometimes complex. As with all groups there tends to be some rules and restrictions but this applies less in non-Wiccan groups. Lone witches often feel they can concentrate and progress better on their own. Their way is usually simpler, more spontaneous and may emphasise herbalism, healing or anything that appeals to the witch. Also trancework is important. In essence the ways are fairly similar, it really is 'horses for courses' but needs a lot of thought. Lone witchcraft is often called 'hedge witchcraft'.

Is paganism the same as witchcraft?

Witchcraft is a type of paganism, but there are many others. Paganism is Nature worship, derived from the Latin *paganus* meaning 'peasant'. Currently it is used as a general term for the resurgence of Goddess-consciousness, green spirituality and respect for the wild and the instinctual. The most well-defined and structured form of paganism today seems to be Wicca.

What is the history of witchcraft?

This is a complex and difficult question. Witchcraft is really about the flight-inspired, about feelings and visions and a certain type of 'consciousness'. Charting the origins and growth of something so abstract is not easy. The factual history is hardly less problematic as historians and scholars continue to argue the matter hotly.

There is evidence to suggest that a mother-goddess was widely worshipped in the Stone Age and that types of magic may have been used to bring about fertility, success in the hunt and other such life basics. Such magic was probably 'sympathetic magic' which means the 'like attracts like' principle. For instance, a hunter who wanted to track down an animal might perform a ritual dance wearing the hide and horns of the animal. Such a rite would also have provided the useful function of forging a psychic bond between hunter and hunted – he could then feel at one with his prey and 'know' where it could be found. Evidence also exists suggesting women held principal power in some ancient cultures. However, all of these matters are in some dispute.

Coming closer to the present brings us to the Celts. Celtic beliefs are important in present-day witchcraft, but I think it is what one might call the 'Celtic mind-set' that is most relevant – poetry and soul and an ever-present sense that the spirit world walks with us, just out of sight at the corner of the eye. The Celtic viewpoint (I generalise here) sees that the 'real' is only one reality and that logic goes only so far – and that sometimes isn't far at all. It seems certain that women did have considerable power in Celtic society – remember Boudicca? – and that clans gathered around influential females. In other words, they were matrifocal.

Evidence of the Celts in Ireland goes back to 12 000 BCE (BCE means Before Common Era – a term preferred by pagans). They had many gods and goddesses, but also worshipped the Great Mother and marked their time around the Moon. In common with present-day pagans they saw no contradiction in sometimes behaving as if there was one Goddess and at other times as if there were many gods and goddesses. From 500 BCE the Celts had become a major force in

 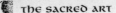

Europe. They have bequeathed the four major fire festivals of Imbolc, Beltane, Lammas and Samhain that we shall be looking at later.

In addition to the Celts, modern witches are influenced by two strands of thought from the Continent, the Apollonian and the Dionysian. Apollo was the Greek Sun god and his cult related to philosophy and the tools of the conscious mind. This influence can be seen to some extent when we compose rituals, but of far more importance to most lone witches is the Dionysian approach. Dionysus was the god of wine, and his cult was ecstatic and wild. His rites were often unstudied and unbridled, more the province of the tangled forest, the moonlit grove. Both approaches sought to raise consciousness, but the inspirational, instinctual Dionysian way is closer to the witch of today, for although we may prepare our rituals in advance we are free to be spontaneous in them and we encourage states of trance and 'merging'.

Isis, the great goddess of ancient Egypt has been called the most complete form of the goddess ever revolved and her worship was widespread and spanned many centuries from the fourth century BCE onwards. The cult of Isis influenced Gnosticism. In the twentieth century occultists associated with the society called the Golden Dawn have recaptured her essence. Notable in this was Dion Fortune in her novels *The Sea Priestess* and *Moon Magic*. There are similarities between the rites of Isis and certain Wiccan ceremonies today, and it is obvious that worship of so great a female deity is inspiring to witches.

The old gods and the different approaches lived comfortably cheek by jowl, for the most part, and magic and its practitioners were accepted as witches, wisewomen and cunning men – indeed, the priestesses and priests were types of witches/magicians in a sense, for they mediated divine mysteries through themselves, rather than by reciting and enforcing creeds. With the advent of Christianity, however, things changed, for intrinsic to the new faith was a total belief that it was the one and only word of God, and slowly the old faiths were stamped out or went underground. Christianity is based on dogma, revealed through one source and disseminated by an ordained priesthood. Some Christian churchmen were anti-women, so it is understandable that such a faith would have been highly uneasy about 'witches'. They are believed to have survived in secret cults of Nature worship, Goddess worship, trance/

19

ecstasy and spell casting, and there is some evidence that certain English kings were part of a 'witch cult'. (I would like to point out that many Christians do not interpret their religion in the way described above and are alive to the message of love brought by Jesus.)

Through the Middle Ages it is really unclear how much witchcraft was practised and some historians say it was virtually none at all. The Renaissance saw a growth in ritual magic. Few magicians were brought to trial because they were usually men of influence – and ritual magic is 'Apollonian' and rather less disturbing to a culture that distrusted personal revelation. The 'witches' were another matter. Exemplifying the power of the Feminine, the non-rational, the instinctual, they could not be tolerated by a masculine, law-giving, God-the-Father oriented religion. Countless numbers were burnt at the stake or hanged (after the Reformation burning was not practised in England). Again I must stress that it is unclear how much 'real' witchcraft was practised, how many of those brought to trial were, in fact, witches by any description and also how many unfortunate people were executed. Some of the picture that has been built up comes from accounts extracted under torture, and so is obviously unreliable.

Kinder times arrived and witchcraft began to be popularised at the end of the nineteenth century and the beginning of the twentieth by writers such as Charles Leland and Margaret Murray, who claimed to be resurrecting old sources. These are discussed in *Paganism for Beginners* but I must say that almost everything they have said has been challenged. Some witches claim to be part of a local or family tradition that goes back through the ages, but strictly speaking the witchcraft that we are considering in this book is a phenomenon of the latter twentieth century, and is really only coming into its own in the final decade, although its roots are undeniably archaic. It is a mixture of ancient lore and tradition and some inspired reconstruction by gifted witches of this century. Most importantly, it stresses the right of each individual witch to find her or his own way by seeking direct experience of the gods. It is a way of dance, dream, poetry and inward soaring.

In the end anyone who practises witchcraft feels no doubt that they are part of something unutterably ancient. It is about rootedness and remembering – memory in the bones, not in the mind. Of course, what we do now is nothing like what a Stone Age woman would have done, wrapped in furs by the side of her fire, and this is only right, for we are

different. And yet we are not so different, really. The Earth still turns, the Sun sets and rises, the breezes play, humans and beasts are born, mate and die – and the witch celebrates the patterns of life, weaves the wind, dreams the dreams of the Goddess into life....

If you choose the way of the witch you will feel that you have come home. Ordinary words strain to describe the experience.

Why are ancient sites so important?

Standing stones, stone circles and ancient earthworks are held by witches to be places of great power, where the energies of the Earth herself are gathered, and may be accessed. However, these forces are powerful and unpredictable, and anyone who seeks to direct them may find they have a tiger by the tail.

Those who are sensitive may find they have dreams and visions stimulated by these places, and some of these experiences can be vivid and life changing. Certainly they are wonderful places for getting the imagination going, and if you write poetry, paint, or just want an interesting picnic they are worth a visit. There are several theories about ancient sites, most of which involve the idea of ley lines – lines of energy on the Earth's crust – which ancient people were aware of and could influence by these structures.

PRACTICE

Visit sacred places, standing stones or tumuli. If there are none close, choose somewhere that feels special to you. Go in early morning or dusk, or perhaps try a mist-shrouded day in autumn. Take note of all you feel and see, perhaps jot it down in a notebook. The importance of just going out, looking and listening, putting your hands on trees and noting how you feel, drinking deep the scents, watching the fluttering, scuttering life in fields and hedgerows, touching soil and grass – this can't be overstated. Collect interesting stones or fallen wood. Also note what you dream the following night, or perhaps on the night before your visit. All this is truly invaluable for finding your magical self. And of course enjoy yourself.

2 MAKING MAGIC

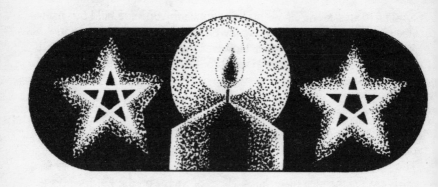

Darksome night and shining moon
East, then south, then west, then north
Harken to the witches' rune
Here we come to call thee forth

Doreen Valiente, *The Witches Rune*

DO WITCHES REALLY DO MAGIC?

Witches do magic. Spirit, emotion, light, sound, feather, petal, stone and bone are vibrations on a spectrum. Witches are very much aware of this interconnectedness. Thoughts are things, but by themselves they are small things. It is rightly said that it's no good wishing. However, the concentration and ritual of magic focus

desire, and enable us to move about the spectrum, so to speak. Working magic is an expression of human will and dignity, for we are moving among the gods, and that is one of the reasons magic has been feared.

Magical consciousness experiences the essential oneness of all things as a reality and it is needed in spellcraft. It is a light trance, an altered state of awareness that is not difficult to achieve with practice. Simply relax, allow a day-dreamy state to grow and the rest will follow. Do not expect anything dramatic, especially at first.

Spells can be likened to prayers. For instance, a person may go into church, light a candle, kneel and say a prayer. That is like a simple spell but instead of begging God to help, the witch will place great importance on her or his own concentration and power – she or he is responsible for the success or failure of the spell. However, no sensible witch believes that such power is the property of the little human ego. Really it comes from the Goddess and the God in all of us.

Most people accept the existence of telepathy and poltergeists, and positive thinking is still a real 'buzz'. All these are a kind of magic. There are levels of reality other than the day-to-day, and more takes place on them than some people realise. During the Second World War a coven of witches in the New Forest in England worked to prevent an invasion by Hitler, who was himself reputed to be using occult forces (the swastika is a magical symbol). Witches are also credited with helping to defeat the Spanish Armada through the storms they whistled up – indeed, Sir Francis Drake himself is said to have been a witch! To many things there is more than meets the eye.

Is magic dangerous?

Anything that is new, and untested can hold dangers if not approached sensibly. Magic is a powerful force and needs to be treated with respect. You would not attempt to go to sea in a cardboard box or wire up a socket without turning off the mains. It is only common sense to use the correct method, whatever you do in life. Learning to ride a bike or to swim is dangerous. Magic is safer than cycling on our busy roads or swimming off our polluted beaches.

Before attempting anything magical, think very carefully about your motives and what it all means to you. Magic is not there to gratify anyone's vanity, although pride in a spell well done is fine. It isn't a game, but neither is it a long-faced matter – the Goddess says 'let there be mirth with reverence'. Approach magic with common sense.

Make sure you are well informed. Read as many books as you can. Perhaps talk to some experienced witches (the Pagan Federation's address is listed at the back of this book). Give magic some real thought. You wouldn't choose a career, move house or even go out in the evening without thinking about it. Magic deserves this.

Get in the habit of visualising a protective circle extending two or three metres around you. Close your eyes and practise picturing this circle of electric blue light. If you are no good at visualising, that does not necessarily matter, but you must feel certain your circle is there. Perhaps you will get a shiver down your spine, as your circle earths itself. Maybe you will get a feeling of safety and security. Perhaps you may hear the sound of your circle of power humming, or even smell its presence, like incense. Whatever method you use is fine as long as you clearly imagine your circle. This circle is the basis of the 'magic circle' so often written about. It is really a sphere, going all round you and the place you are working. It will protect you as you open yourself to do magic, and prevent you feeling depleted. Please be sure you always use your protective circle whenever attempting anything magical, and disperse it when you have finished. Full instructions are given for the ritual of the magic circle in Chapter 6.

Always steer well clear of anyone or anything that doesn't feel quite right. People who are up to no good are usually transparent.

There is another consideration – something that Shan, in her book *Circlework* (see 'Further Reading') calls the 'magic mirror'. What this means is that when we begin to set magical forces in motion we activate unconscious, or barely conscious elements in ourselves – and these may come back at us in frightening experiences. Many of us are brought up riddled with guilt and doubts, although we may reject this consciously. Indeed, if we have been badly messed up we may reject what we have been taught all the more emphatically. It may seem doubly violating that these unpleasant beliefs are still part of us.

If this is you, do please do yourself a favour and think carefully about what I say. In denying what is a part of you, you really are repeating a destructive pattern. These things are not easily eliminated – how could they be? If something has formed the fabric of your life, if it has been dinned into you by parents and teachers that you loved, respected or feared then in a way it is a part of you – for now. By lovingly accepting this and working with it you will come to bring these unpleasant factors out into daylight, see how they are operating in your life and be able to deal with them. This does take a while. So give yourself the time you need – you owe that to yourself.

Do witches harm people by magic?

The answer to this is definitely no, for several reasons. The 'boomerang' effect states that what you do comes back to you threefold, so who is going to risk that? More importantly, the very idea of harming anyone is out of keeping with the life-affirming nature of the Craft. A true magical working demands a lot from the witch, and a bad spell is a horrid thing to attempt. Magic is a positive thing. If we have been sacked, a spell to get us a new – and better – job is likely to cheer us up, and get results. Wishing our boss would catch a virus in his lap-top will just make things worse for us. 'Live well is the best revenge.'

It is a mistake to imagine we are at the mercy of anything malevolent that might come our way. We all have a psychic 'skin' to keep out anything that might seek to harm. This can be strengthened by regularly forming our magic circle. Of course, there are occasional scary stories put about by people who believe they have been harmed by black magic. The key word is 'believe'. If you believe you are being harmed then your fears will work against you in a negative magic of your own. The best antidote is to try to think positively, get plenty of fresh air – and find someone understanding to talk it all over with. Inevitably there are the occasional unpleasant types who meddle with magic. Keep well away from them, and follow the words of the Goddess when She says 'Keep pure your highest ideal. Strive ever towards it. Let naught stop you or turn you aside.'

Isn't magic contrary to the rules of science?

Well – yes, and no. Magic really operates outside the realms for which conventional science has rules. Of course, there are those who will say that if science hasn't defined and labelled something then it doesn't exist, or at least can't be taken seriously. That view is unimaginative, to say the least. It denies meaningful experience and can bar the way to progress. It would also seem to ignore the new science that is emerging, and will no doubt be as natural to the twenty-first century as Newtonian ways of looking at things are to us. Of course, we know Einstein's theory of relativity is a twentieth-century development, but this hasn't really been absorbed into general thinking. (It is worth noting here that Newton, the giant intellect, was deeply mystical and regarded his spiritual work as much more important than the scientific problems which he solved with a dash of the 'lion's paw'.)

There are several developments in recent thought that are generally supportive of magic. For instance, there is the theory of 'synchronicity' advanced by the psychologist C G Jung. Put simply, this attests that there can be connections between events that are something other than cause and effect. Witches know this instinctively, and their art is the manipulation of these 'synchronous connections'.

Arthur Koestler wrote (in *The Sleepwalkers*, Pelican, 1984): '...it is meaningless to ask at what precise point of its orbit the electron is at a given moment of time. It is equally everywhere'. He also quotes the scientist James Jeans '"...the universe begins to look more like a great thought than a great machine"'. So our ideas of space and time are not 'real'. 'Reality' becomes ever more elusive to the science of today. It seems science is drawing close to the realms of magic. Certain scientific experiments on subatomic particles have even shown that they appear to be affected by the mind of the experimenter. Such ideas are explored by writers, for example Colin Wilson in his works *The Occult, Mysteries* and others. If the Universe is 'a great thought' then it can surely be influenced by thought.

Finally, the evolving 'chaos theory' brings physics and mathematics together and explores the patterns of complex systems for which conventional science has no effective rules (e.g. the movements of a fast-spinning waterwheel). This has given rise to the entrancing idea of the Butterfly Effect – if a butterfly's wings stir the air in Peking it can cause storms in New York next month. For 'butterfly's wings' you might substitute 'magic wand', except that what happens when the wand is in the hand of a concentrating and experienced practitioner is not haphazard.

So if you have logical teeth needing something to chew, there are a few bones! Magic is of the heart. It is not of the 'reality' we call scientific, but a healthy scepticism is to be recommended, for sceptics make better witches.

Does magic work?

In a word, yes, but not always exactly as we have in mind, for magic changes the person who works it. Real magical transformation takes place in the mind of the practitioner, which then translates to changes in the physical world. These changes come through ordinary means and are rarely dramatic. A properly worked spell will always have some effect, but success is sometimes partial and may come about in ways we have not anticipated. Transformations take place gently, in the ordinary course of things. It is just the witch who says a quiet 'Ah-ha'.

There is an interesting thought about working magic: many people are drawn to witchcraft, to a greater or lesser extent because they hope they will be able to get what they want – whatever that may be. However, the altered consciousness necessary for working magic quite often makes the goal itself seem less relevant or crucial. Everything looks different. Sometimes it seems one already has all one could possibly wish for. Maybe that is why many witches are not rich – it just doesn't really matter. After all, the true goal of magical working is heightened awareness and union with the Goddess and the God.

how does magic work?

Magic works through the power of the mind, using the imagination to build up a clear picture of what is worked for and sending the image forth to do its work. It requires a high degree of concentration and the ability to visualise clearly and exclusively, for what may be quite long periods – ritual helps the process. It also involves the raising of power to energise the spell.

Since time immemorial occultists have spoken of the 'astral plane'. This is a subtle plane existing alongside the everyday – it can be thought of as a world of finer essence. It is the stuff of thoughts and dreams and we can enter it nightly. Dreams may be partly remembered astral travelling, for we all have an 'astral body' that interpenetrates our physical body, but often separates when we sleep. Some people are able to astral travel consciously and the old stories about witches' 'flying ointment' and wild journeys through the air (on broomsticks) are really accounts of astral travel. (Another interpretation of broomstick-riding may be flying astride a branch of the 'world tree' called *Yggdrasil* in Norse mythology. The world tree is central to many cosmological maps, joining lower, middle and upper worlds, and used by Shamans on their journeys.) It is on this astral plane that magical effects first take shape, translating them to physical reality. However, physical actions need to back up magical actions. All the spells in the world won't get you a job unless you send off applications.

how does a witch raise power?

This can be done in a variety of ways and sometimes it doesn't seem necessary to raise power as such – simply concentrating hard may be all that is needed. Power can be raised by chanting, dancing, drumming or rhythmic gesture. This also has the effect of dulling the conscious mind and helps to create a light trance helpful for magic. The power can rise in a cone shape, and at the correct moment has to be directed towards its purpose. The power thus raised comes from the delicate electrical currents of the human body and consciousness is heightened in the practitioner.

WhAT IS A chANT?

This is a rhyme, also called a rune, intoned rhythmically to raise power. Such rhymes can be simple and repetitive – indeed it's probably best they are – and they need to scan and rhyme well, so they trip off the tongue. Lone witches will often make up their own. Here is an example of a power chant. Of course, there are longer – and better – chants available.

> Pentacle and Earth and North
> Call the cone of magic forth
> Air and East, athame bright
> Cone of magic to its height
> Fire and South and candle burn
> Make the cone of magic turn
> Cauldron deep and West and Water
> Cone of magic never falter
> Aya, aya Anu, aya, aya Lugh
> Aya, aya Anu, aya, aya Lugh

The last two lines can be repeated as often as necessary – a sense for this develops naturally. Anu is a Celtic name for the Great Mother Goddess. Lugh (pronounced 'Loo') again is Celtic and means 'shining one'. He was god of the Sun, crafting and harvesting. The names are chosen for their sound as much as anything else.

Why IS vISUALISATION SO IMPORTANT?

By visualisation (i.e. by the force of clear imagination), we create the reality of our spell. We need to be able to see our magical goals become real, with precision and detail, and so we are setting up the power circuit for our spell. Some people do find it impossible to visualise in the sense of seeing their goal. I do not think this prevents them from working magic. However, in some way the intention of the spell has to become an inner reality for the witch for the magic to take effect. Goals need to be formulated clearly by other means – props may be useful for this, such as pictures or personal effects.

How does a witch cast a spell?

I am sure each witch has her or his own way of going about things. Also some of the steps are quite subtle and natural, and only discovered by practice – which, as they say, makes prefect! I'll give an account of the basics.

First, you need to feel good about the whole business, and that could be affected by lots of things. The phase of the Moon is important. Also you need to make sure that you won't be disturbed. Night-time is often best.

Having decided to start, assemble the equipment for the ritual and put on the garment you usually wear, or go naked, for many witches like to work nude. You may like to meditate for a while, especially if this work is especially important. Allow consciousness to alter to the magical consciousness. Then ritually cleanse your working area and cast your magic circle. We have already spoken of the magic circle, but the full ceremony is explained later in this book.

The Elements, which correspond to the four compass points are also invoked at the appropriate points around the circle – the quartered circle was a favourite Celtic design. This is an important concept, because elements and directions represent our Earthly state, they ground us and protect us and they represent different energies that we need and work with. North is equated with Earth, East with Air, South with Fire and West with Water, although this is sometimes rotated through 180 degrees in the southern hemisphere.

'Invoke' means to cause to appear inwardly, as opposed to 'evoke' which is an external apparition – magicians evoke spirits. We would not presume to attempt to evoke Elements or god-forms. The presence of an aspect of the Goddess or God may also be called upon. For instance, if your working was to be about pregnancy or creativity you might think of the Great Mother as Isis, Brighid or Demeter.

Clearly state the intention of the work. You should have formulated it earlier, before creating the circle, when thought was clear and logical. Now you can raise power by chanting or dancing, direct it, complete your spell and release it. Finally, some form of communion

with the Goddess and God rounds off the ritual, with thanks, and farewell. The circle is now allowed to fade. Ground yourself consciously, perhaps by eating or drinking. To get a full idea of how to go about this, you should study other chapters, so that you know about symbols, magical tools and such like.

What different sorts of spells are there?

There are many, many types of spell. Some use candles, some use thread, wax images, stones, potions – the list is endless. Some spells use almost nothing but a great deal of willpower and visualising, and these are sometimes the most difficult.

Before setting about magic seriously, you should do work with dreams and trance, and you should have been initiated in some form. We look at initiation later on. There is no harm in a less formal approach, however, for simple matters, so below are some examples.

General spell to improve life

(N.B. this is an adaptable spell, but you should be clear about the specific improvement you want when you do it.)

Pick a candle and joss stick of the appropriate colour and type for your spell – see the next question for advice on this. Make sure you're not going to be disturbed for the next half hour or so. Light your joss stick, close the curtains, do whatever you need to do to get in the mood for your spell – close your eyes, breathe evenly, enter 'magical consciousness'. Keep matches by you and a blunt knife, if your nails are short.

Visualise your magic circle – take your time with this. When you feel ready turn towards the North (roughly, you don't need a compass). This is the realm of the Powers of Earth. Their gifts are common sense, practicality, groundedness, material achievement. Think about these gifts. Imagine also green fields, hills, stones, mountains, caves. Thank the Earth spirits for being present.

Turn then towards the East, the home of the Powers of Air. Communication, clear and swift thought, freedom, intellectuality, smooth movement – these are the gifts of Air. Think about these. Imagine fresh winds on a mountain peak, flying, morning light. Thank the Air spirits for being present.

Now turn South, towards the Powers of Fire. Passion, spontaneity, energy, enterprise, intuition and inspiration are their gifts. Think of these and imagine sunlight, bonfires, fireworks, wild dances, warmth. Thank the Fire spirits for being present.

Lastly turn to the West and the Powers of Water. Empathy, compassion, caring, nurturing, imagination and dreams, love and understanding – these are the gifts of Water. Think of these, imagine streams, lakes, the ocean and the soft coolness of water. Thank the Water spirits for being present.

Pick up your candle and hold it up in the direction most appropriate to your purpose. For instance, if you want more direction in your career both North and South could be suitable. For success in exams East would be the choice. If your health needs to improve West could be the direction, although extra energy would come from the South. If you need consoling in a sorrow or seek love, again choose West, although the South would be the home of passion. Choose what feels right, you don't have to be pedantic. Visualise the power or quality streaming into the candle. Use your nail or the blunt knife to engrave your initial on the candle, or better still mark it with a pentagram, which is a five-pointed star. Light the candle and say:

> *Candle flame, candle burn,*
> *See the wheel of my life turn*
> *Candle burn, candle bright,*
> *Turn me now towards the light*

Say this three times. Give yourself a few minutes for contemplation. Perhaps light another joss stick. When you are ready, thank each of the Elements in turn, snuff out the candle and allow your circle to fade. Now you have your special candle. Make sure you light it each day and repeat the chant three times, until the candle is burnt down and/or you have your wish.

MIRROR SPELL

This spell is given in *Witchcraft for Tomorrow* by Doreen Valiente (Hale, 1978). For this you will need a small mirror and joss stick/ incense. Two candles, of appropriate colour if possible, and matches (believe me it's all too easy to forget these!).

Again ensure peace and quiet. Draw the curtains – when the candles are lit there should be just enough light to see your face. Create your magic circle by strongly visualising it. Light incense and candles.

Now look into the mirror and concentrate upon the desired wish. Concentrate your eyes upon the reflection of your eyes. Then close your eyes and be still. Develop the image of your wish in your mind, and when you have visualised it clearly open your eyes. Again concentrate hard upon the eyes in the mirror, trying to look through them into a space beyond. Whisper the wish three times. Light another joss stick or burn more incense, if you wish. Contemplate for a moment. Close your ritual and allow the circle to fade. This spell can also be used to build self-confidence by talking to oneself, in the mirror, as if to a third party.

ANGER SPELL

(This is given by Starhawk in *The Spiral Dance*.)

This spell needs to be done alongside flowing water – I suggest in a private corner surrounded by bushes at the side of a stream.

Create your magic circle. Cup a black stone in your hands and raise it to your forehead. Concentrate and send all your anger into the stone. Do this for as long as you can, until you can do it no longer. Then hurl the stone with all your might into the water and say:

> With this stone
> Anger be gone
> Water bind it
> No-one find it

Place your palms upon the ground for a few moments to earth the power and allow your circle to fade. Now go home and take care of

yourself for you may feel depleted for a while, but you will be better later. Alternatively, you may feel great straight away.

What are magical 'correspondences'?

Lists of correspondences can be extensive. They appear in the Qabalah (see Chapter 4), but there are other systems. 'Correspondences' is the word used for all sorts of things – colours, numbers, plants, creatures, compass points, concepts – that have an affinity with each other. In other words, they harmonise. They are used in magic on the principle that 'like attracts like' and so for spells a witch would choose colours, stones or whatever that are in keeping with the purpose. Remember, these are traditions, not dogmas, and traditions do vary somewhat. So respect traditions, follow your feelings and 'if in doubt, leave it out'. Below is a list of correspondences for certain spells.

Love, beauty, youth, joy, happiness, reconciliation, pleasure, friendship, compassion, mediation

Venus, Aphrodite, Freya. Green (possibly soft rose or blue). Rose, vanilla, ylang-ylang, thyme, mint. Emerald, lapis lazuli, turquoise (also rose quartz – this stone is principally associated with the Moon, but the Moon can also be appropriate in love magic). The signs Taurus and Libra (N.B. joss sticks are often labelled for zodiac sign so pick accordingly for spells). Doves, swans. The tarot card The Empress. Friday.

The home, fertility, family, healing, gardening, meaningful dreams and spirituality (also love)

The Moon, The Great Mother, Brigid, Dana, Levanah. White or silver. Calamus, jasmine, lotus, willow, gardenia, lemon balm, coconut. Aquamarine, chalcedony, quartz, moonstone, mother-of-pearl. The sign Cancer. Fish and dolphins. The dog, the bear, the snake and all

animals with crescent-shaped horns have been associated with the Moon. Tarot card The High Priestess. Monday.

Health, protection, legal matters, enlightenment, success and energy in magic and physical matters

The Sun, Apollo, Lugh, Ra. Orange or gold. Bay, benzoin, copal, frankincense, cinnamon, orange, carnation, sandalwood (also associated with the Moon), rosemary. Amber, carnelian, diamond, tiger's eye, sunstone. The sign Leo. Lion, sparrowhawk. Tarot card The Sun. Sunday.

Strengthen intelligence, eloquence, study, communication, travel, self-improvement, divination, wisdom

Mercury, Woden/Odin Thoth. Yellow. Carraway, almond, fennel, dill, lavender, peppermint. Agate, aventurine, mottled jasper. The signs Gemini and Virgo. Monkeys, swallows. Tarot card The Magician. Wednesday.

Courage, assertion, healing (after surgery), strength, sexuality, defensive magic and exorcism

Mars, Ares, Thor. Red. Wormwood, ginger, dragon's blood, cumin, coriander, basil, galangal. Bloodstone, flint, red jasper, garnet, ruby, red tourmaline. The sign Aries (and Scorpio, especially for moral courage, exorcism, sexuality). The ram, scorpion, horse. Tarot card The Tower. Thursday.

Prosperity, legal settlements, spiritual and religious matters, psychism and meditation

Jupiter, Zeus, Tiw/Tir. Purple – possibly 'royal' blue. Sage, ti, nutmeg, maple, honeysuckle, clove. Amethyst, lepidolite. The sign Sagittarius

– also Pisces. The centaur, horse, eagle. Tarot card The Wheel of Fortune. Tuesday.

BINDING, GROUNDING, CENTRING, PROTECTING, PURIFYING AND CERTAIN KINDS OF LUCK, SOMETIMES FERTILISING AND NURTURING

Saturn, Chronos, sometimes The Horned God. Brown, black, grey (sometimes dark green). Cypress, patchouli, tamarisk, comfrey, pansy, amaranth, yew. Apache tear, jet, onyx, obsidian. The sign Capricorn – also Aquarius. Goat, horned animals. Tarot card The World. Saturday.

As an example, to promote clear thinking for an exam, we might do our spell on a Wednesday, burning an incense of lavender, dill and fennel. Our candles would be yellow, and we might spread a length of yellow silk out upon the altar or working site. Perhaps we might also have a piece of agate with us, for magical charging. But do remember that significances overlap. Keep it simple. Go with what feels right and what evokes a suitable response in you.

PRACTICE

There have been several things to practise in this chapter. You may try out one of the spells, or learn the power chant – make up one of your own if you prefer. Most important, regularly practise forming your magic, protective circle.

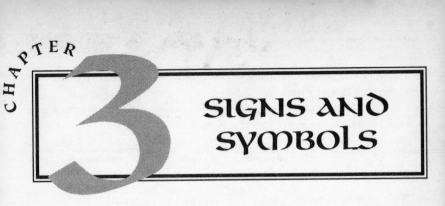

SIGNS AND SYMBOLS

...a word or an image is symbolic when it implies something more than its obvious and immediate meaning.... As the mind explores the symbol, it is led to ideas that lie beyond the grasp of reason...

C G Jung, *Man and his Symbols*

Why are symbols important?

It has been said that a picture paints a thousand words, and the same can be said of many symbols. Powerful symbols activate a chain of associations in the mind. Like a hall of mirrors, the images evoked seem to stretch way back into distant memory and can provoke a gut reaction that we all seem to share.

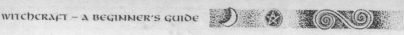

Because of their many associations symbols can bring about a change in consciousness. The occultist Dion Fortune called magic 'the art of producing changes of consciousness at will'. Part of the skill of spell-working is the ability to shift one's perceptions. This helps to bring about the magical effects that the witch is seeking. Thus certain symbols are most important in the working of magic.

What does the spiral mean?

This signifies an inward journey, so it can mean initiation and subtle knowledge. It also represents the emergence into consciousness of what was formerly hidden – the double spiral means descent and return. The spiral also suggests the round of the seasons, where life unfolds, fades, unfolds again in a repeating circle – it means life itself. Witches often dance in a spiral, echoing this.

What does the pentagram mean?

The pentagram, or five-pointed star, is perhaps the sign most often linked to witchcraft. It symbolises the four elements, Earth, Water, Air and Fire, plus the fifth 'element' ether, or spirit. It is usually shown with a single point uppermost, meaning the power of the mind working creatively with matter. With an apex pointing downwards it looks like the face of a goat, and has been associated with the seeking of control for dubious purposes. But this really only

pentagram or five-point star

means the spiritual spark hidden within matter, and the poor goat is, after all, a useful and fertile animal!

Sometimes the pentagram is seen as representing the sacred Feminine, as it looks like the spreadeagled body of a woman. It is a favourite decoration for witches, and many wear it on a ring or necklace. As a pentacle, or disk, it appears on Wiccan altars, signifying Earth.

Being able to trace a pentagram in the air is useful in magic, and it is much used by Wiccans. To invoke the Earth element (and generally as an invoking sign) the pentagram is traced starting at the top apex, going down to the left, up to the right, and so on. Finally, repeat the

earth-invoking pentagram.

initial stroke. For banishing, start at the bottom left point, go upwards and proceed similarly. The invoking pentagram is useful for general use, such as consecrating wine. The banishing pentagram may be used when confronted by anything unpleasant, perhaps when in deep trance or Qabalistic pathworking (discussed in Chapter 4) or in

earth-banishing pentagram.

banishing spells. This can be borne in mind, but does not concern us here.

What does the ankh mean?

The ankh is a loop, or circle, placed on top of a T. It is associated with ancient Egypt, although it is probably older even than that, and some say it is linked with Atlantis. It means Life, the loop being the Feminine and the T-shape being the Masculine, which together generate existence. It also suggests a key, and is a symbol for initiation. Many witches like to wear an ankh.

·ankh·

What does the hexagram mean?

The hexagram, or six-pointed star, has also been called the Star or Seal of Solomon. It can symbolise the spreadeagled male body. Composed of two equilateral triangles, it also means balance between Masculine and Feminine – a recurring theme! The upward pointing triangle signifies Man, while the downward pointing means Woman – the triangles of Fire and Water, respectively. It has associations with ritual magic and the Qabalah, with more complex meanings that are outside the scope of this book. (This applies equally to other symbols.)

·Star of Solomon·

WHAT ABOUT TRIANGLES, CIRCLES AND CROSSES?

The triangle pointing upwards (like a bonfire) can mean Fire and Masculine, whereas pointing downwards (like a chalice) it suggests Water and Feminine. It is also used for evocation (i.e. the calling up of spirits) in ritual magic. The triangle is drawn separate from the magic circle, so that the magician is protected, and can command the spirit from a safe position. This is generally outside the domain of witches and their craft.

Three is sometimes held to be the number of Manifestation, a creative duo giving rise to a third: father, mother and child. There are many trinities of Gods and Goddess – notably the Triple Goddess, of course.

Four is the number of Matter – the four Elements, dimensions, points of the compass. These are important as they represent where and what we are. The quartered circle represents the Earthly state. There are four major festivals, or sabbats, marking the round of the seasons and our connection with the world of matter, as we shall see in Chapter 7.

The circle is a symbol of eternity, perfection, and also protection. It is the most symmetrical mathematical shape. with no ends or corners. It is regularly used by witches who construct a magic circle, or sphere, for their workings.

Celtic Cross or quartered circle

What is an amulet?

This is an object carried for general good luck. An example of this might be a holey stone or stone found with a hole in the centre, probably caused by the action of water. These are often taken to symbolise the Goddess. The four-leaf clover is also lucky, and if you find one you should press it and keep it for good fortune. Other examples are lucky pennies, rabbits' feet, medals, and so on.

What is a talisman?

An amulet is for general good fortune, but a talisman is a charm for a specific purpose – for example to attract love, to be able to think more clearly, to be more successful at making money, etc. The making of talismans is part of the art of the witch, so it is worthwhile looking at this in some detail.

Some knowledge of correspondences is helpful – we looked at these in Chapter 2. Having said this, the village witch of old would probably have gone by instinct in this, as in other matters, and it isn't a bad idea to trust our own.

Let us imagine that a lonely friend comes to us for help in attracting love. She is recently divorced, and can't seem to form new attachments. Part of the role of the 'wisewoman' would be to talk this through with her, for there will almost certainly be some

blockage within her that is preventing her attracting affection. Is she bitter and angry? Does she secretly blame all men for her plight? Does she feel guilty, unworthy, afraid? Is she worried how her teenage son would react if she had a boyfriend? All these may need to be considered, for a good witch needs also to be something of a counsellor. Magic won't work nearly so well – if at all – if there is something unacknowledged in the mind that is keeping it out (although with precise knowledge some spells could help dissolve such blocks). So a witch who is serious about helping needs to be an earnest student of human nature. This may need training and a fair bit of experience, for potted psychology can serve only to irritate further those who are already bruised.

Homily over! Let's get back to our talisman. You decide that you will make a talisman to help your friend draw towards her the affection she needs. For this, you will need some sturdy paper or card (plain postcards are good, but you will need to cut off the printed bits) a pencil, some coloured crayons or felt-tips and a pair of scissors. Cut out the shape you want for your talisman. The circle is a good general shape. Think about what you are trying to achieve. It is caring love, not sizzling passion which might be a bit over the top for your vulnerable friend. What do you associate with the idea of love? Let us start with Venus, planet and goddess most often linked with love and relationships (passion is Mars). Venus colours are green and rose, also soft blue. Flowers are roses (surprise, surprise), daisies, violets. Herbs are mint and thyme. Soft fruits may be Venus fruits. For our purpose here the apple could be a good choice. When you bisect an apple at right angles to the core you find that the centre looks like a five-pointed star. Doves and swans are Venus birds and the elder is often associated with Venus. Perhaps we have enough to be going along with!

What you put on your talisman will depend on how artistic you are and how much time you have to spare. You could draw the planetary symbol for Venus and cut an apple cross-wise, dab it on an ink pad and put the imprint of the little star at the centre of your talisman. You may think of other symbols. You will need to personalise your talisman for your friend. Actually writing her name is a bit obvious, so perhaps you could include the symbol for her zodiac sign. Maybe

she has characteristics or preferences that you could show symbolically, or you could use a fingerprint or strand of hair. Do what feels right.

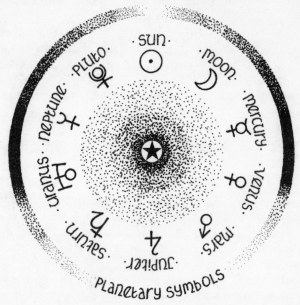

Planetary symbols

When you have completed your talisman you will need to consecrate it. You may do this simply by holding it between your palms, closing your eyes and letting a feeling of love well up in your chest. When you are ready pour this into the talisman with as much power as you are capable of. When you are more used to magical workings you may prefer to do this more formally, in a proper magic circle, with incense and candles, raising power in your preferred way and directing it to the talisman. The latter is best, but either can work – I am sure the witches of old often had to work quickly! If you are a beginner, however, do make sure that you have peace and quiet and the right atmosphere for what you are doing. Mentally construct your protective circle before you begin.

Finally give the talisman to your friend, preferably wrapped in a piece of natural cloth coloured green or rose, and tell her to keep it with her at all times, next to her skin if possible.

What is a 'Book of Shadows'?

This is the name given to the magical diary or notebook, kept by most witches – although word of mouth sufficed for centuries. In Wiccan covens it is usual for initiates to copy out of the Book of Shadows of the High Priestess as part of their training. This will obviously contain details of Wiccan lore.

The 'Book of Shadows' is so called because it is a secret book. Also what is written can only ever be a 'shadow' of the actual magic worked. Not all witches will use this term, however. 'Book of Illumination' might fit just as well, or any other appealing title. In it a witch records details of trancework, plans for rituals, poems, dreams, ideas about the God and Goddess, symbols – in short, whatever seems important for magical development.

How does astrology connect with witchcraft?

I should make it clear that many astrologers would take a dim view of being linked with witchcraft, for they wish their subject to be recognised as a science. Any connection with witches could be seen as a backward step, and that is their privilege.

Knowledge of astrology can be helpful to the witch when selecting the best time for magical workings. At the very least astrology used by the witch is knowledge of the Moon's phases. Spells to increase and grow are best undertaken with a waxing Moon, whereas a 'wanion' or spell to banish is favoured by the waning Moon. The Full Moon is a powerful time for magic of all sorts, and to bring matters to a culmination.

Witches may also take into account the sign occupied by the Sun, as that is easily found out from magazines. The witch may decide to concentrate on home and emotional subjects when in a water sign (Cancer, Scorpio, Pisces), on practical things and money in earth (Capricorn, Taurus, Virgo), intellect and communication in air

(Aquarius, Gemini, Libra), and on enterprise, inspiration and career in the fire signs (Sagittarius, Leo, Aries). However, for magic the sign position of the Moon is usually more important, and a witch who is also something of an astrologer will be able to find out the current Moon sign from planetary tables, also called an ephemeris.

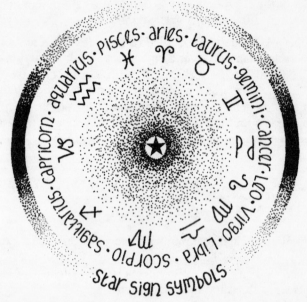

Star sign symbols

In addition, the position of the planets needs to be taken into consideration. For instance, it would be inadvisable to do a spell for successful study while Mercury, the planet of intellect, forms a stressful angle with, say, Saturn, planet of restriction. The influence of transiting planets on the witch's own birth horoscope might also be significant.

Thus astrology can be highly relevant to witchcraft. There is evidence to suggest that our ancient forefathers and mothers took the positions of the planets into account when making use of Earth energies. This is a knowledge that would hardly have been within the reach of the illiterate witch of the more recent past, however. Certainly no-one should become 'astrology-ridden'. Intuition is as good a guide as any planetary tables.

PRACTICE

Practise some of the things described in this chapter. You may like to practise making a talisman and do some more research of your own into correspondences and how you feel about them – your impressions are most important, so take time to form them and be clear about them. Also practise tracing the pentagrams described in the air with your finger. In this way you are learning a bit of useful ritual.

4

THINGS WITCHES DO

I dance with you in
the House of the Weavers
I step the weft
I walk the warp
I dance the spiral round

Carolyn Hillyer, 'House of the Weavers', from the album *House of the Weavers* and the book *Two Drumbeats: Songs of the Sacred Earth* (Seventh Wave Music, 1993)

Why is Ritual important?

Ritual is a set of symbolic actions that brings about an inner transformation. Religious and magical rituals are designed to alter our state of consciousness, to heighten awareness and increase a sense of 'connectedness' – for magic works on the principle that

all is connected. Ritual should be meaningful to us, and so anything that doesn't feel right can be abandoned. However, the bedrock of ritual is tradition. We know in our bones what is built on ancestral rock and we resonate to it.

Can witches tell the future?

Clairvoyance and witchcraft do not necessarily go together, although most witches are intuitive, and use forms of divination.

What forms of divination do witches use?

Scrying – looking for images in a crystal or bowl of water (see page 52) – is often employed. And tarot cards are popular. You can read more about this in *Tarot for Beginners* in this series. Of course, there are many other forms of divination. Remember to keep a sense of proportion and humour. Often questions are not answered directly because they are not as important as we think for our life path. And symbols like skulls don't necessarily mean disaster – a skull could mean ancestral wisdom. So keep an open mind.

Why are herbs and oils important in witchcraft?

They are important for their organic qualities and also for their 'correspondences'. They have mystical powers of their own, and we can learn from them for they convey a rich spectrum of experience through the sense of smell. Incense is especially important in creating the right atmosphere and altering the state of consciousness. You can buy blends of incense, but equally you can make your own. Choose substances in keeping with your purpose – you will find a few hints on this in the list of correspondences we looked at in Chapter 2. Traditions suggest combining ingredients in

threes or multiples thereof. Remember, incense does not have to smell 'nice' to be effective. Magic and ritual are always best accompanied by incense, so make sure you have a joss stick or two at the very least. You can burn combustible incense in a censer, on charcoal, or in a bowl containing sand. You can often buy such articles where you buy the incense.

What is the importance of ritual tools?

Witches use a variety of ritual tools, such as the wand and the chalice, for several reasons. They are a focus for concentration and visualisation. You can imagine a stream of power emanating from a wand. The power is coming from you, not the wand, but it helps your single-mindedness. Also ritual tools help the working of magic because their symbolic meaning is imprinted deeply on the mind. Looking at them helps visualisation and to focus state of mind. After constant use this association becomes even stronger, so that touching and laying out your equipment is an important part of preparing for spellwork and achieving the right consciousness. Artefacts have their own mysterious power, too, by virtue of essence or shape.

Wand Used to conjure and direct energy. It is associated with South and Fire. It is traditionally the length of the user's forearm, from fingertip to elbow, and preferably made from fallen wood. If you cut the wood, ask permission of the tree and thank it afterwards. Wands are represented in fairy stories as having sparks coming from the tip. For me this is irresistibly linked to Fire.

Candle Connected to South and Fire.

Athame (ath-AY-mee) A knife, which must be blunt and never used to cut anything. It is used similarly to the wand. I think of the athame as something to direct concentration, whereas the wand confers inspiration and invocation. The athame is associated with East and Air, although some traditions reverse the meanings of wand and athame, associating the latter with fire. The 'cutting' symbolism of the knife relates to the intellect's cutting edge.

Incense Associated with the Air element.

Pentacle A disk with a pentagram on it that represents Earth and North.

Stones Can be placed on the working site to symbolise Earth

Cauldron and **chalice** Linked with West and Water. Fire and Air are considered Masculine while Earth and Water are Feminine. The chalice and the cauldron are obvious female symbols, both representing the womb and the female ability to contain and nurture. The chalice is used for consecrated drinks such as wine or fruit juice. The cauldron used to be used to make brews. It can be filled with water and used for scrying, to contain a candle as a small ritual fire, or for any purposes the ritual demands. Cauldrons can be three-legged – representing the Triple Goddess – or more usually four-legged, representing the four elements. The cauldron of the goddess Cerridwen was the Cauldron of Wisdom, Transmutation, Regeneration and Enlightenment; thus it is linked to birth, death and rebirth. In a cauldron separate bits of food are combined to form a stew. In the womb – a type of cauldron – sperm and egg are combined to form a baby. Thus the cauldron is a vessel of transformation: what comes out is greater than the sum of the parts that went in. Because of this it has also been linked to the fifth element, ether or spirit.

In medieval times poor people would have used household objects for magic, but I feel that it is better to keep ritual tools separate if possible, for then they are more special. Other traditional tools of the witch are the **white-handled knife** for cutting herbs (although I think scissors are more sensible for most uses) and the **besom**, or broomstick, which is used ritually to cleanse the working area.

WHAT IS A TRANCE?

A trance is an altered state of consciousness, but there is nothing mysterious about it. Everyone goes through a type of trance twice a day, as they wake up and as they go to sleep, and being deeply absorbed in a book induces a light trance. Meditation, pathworking

and trance are used almost interchangeably to mean inner journeys, and these are important for they confer knowledge. Witchcraft is a shamanic religion, relying on personal revelation and the visionary. Trance is the way to this. An example is given in Chapter 9. Complex things are written about trance, but it is a very natural state. Doing it at will just means learning to control and direct what you do many times daily, i.e. day-dreaming. Of course, some will get the hang of it more quickly and will achieve deep trance more readily, but anyone can become proficient with practice.

What is scrying?

Scrying needs the state of light trance called 'magical consciousness'. This is both concentration and relaxation at once. Let your mind drift as it does before going to sleep, free of all thoughts. You may need to keep trying until you find the state of mind that works for you. Often scrying is best attempted by candlelight or moonlight, when all is quiet.

'Crystal gazing' is the best publicised form of scrying, but you can use almost any surface that reflects and into which you can gaze deeply. Many semi-precious stones are suitable, a dark mirror (which is a piece of glass, usually convex, coated with black paint on the back) or simply a bowl or cauldron of water. You can drop a silver coin or ring kept especially for magical purposes into the water if you like a point of light to be reflected, or you may prefer the surface to be dark.

Practice, patience and experiment are important, so you discover the conditions that work for you. Don't give up at the first attempt. If you are unsuccessful at first, try and try again until eventually you succeed. If nothing happens after half an hour abandon your attempt, and try again at another time, another lunar phase or whatever. Gaze into your glass or water and eventually what you are looking at will seem to disappear and images will form in your mind, although some people actually 'see' pictures. Make a note of what you see, but do not jump to conclusions about meanings, for these may be symbolic.

WHAT IS CONSECRATION?

Consecration means dedication to some sacred purpose. Witches often like to consecrate their magical tools, and this can be done simply, perhaps by passing the object through incense smoke, visualising the purpose for which it is intended, and saying 'I consecrate this ... for .... May it serve me well and harm none. In the name of the God and the Goddess. So mote it be. ('Mote' is an old English word, meaning 'must', frequently used by witches.) Wine or cake can be consecrated to the Goddess and one way of doing this is to insert the tip of the athame, describing a pentagram in wine, and saying 'Blessed be this food (wine) unto my body. May it confer health and strength, in the holy name of the Goddess.' These are examples.

DO WITCHES DO HEALING?

The village wisewoman was probably a counsellor, healer and midwife. Today, witches are often in the healing professions. Also witches tend to do 'spiritual healing' of some sort, through laying-on hands, spells, herbs, etc. This is a whole subject in itself, and although it is important, we cannot do more than mention it here. In particular, witches work to heal the earth, for the harm we are doing to her indicates the distortions in our culture. Even if we as a species do not destroy Gaia herself, we could make her tragically inhospitable to us, and to others.

DO WITCHES TAKE DRUGS?

There are a few who do, in order to produce states of deep trance. The witches of old used drugs, sometimes called 'flying ointment' and drugs are sometimes used in shamanism – although in Siberia a shaman who took drugs was considered to be 'second rate'. Of course, we all know taking drugs can be very dangerous.

Do witches take note of their dreams?

Most do, for dreams convey messages. Only by noting dreams regularly can their whole scale of meanings become clearer, and they can be useful in magic and ritual.

Dream interpretation is not a simple matter. There are some good books available on interpreting the symbols in dreams (there is one in this series). They can be stimulating to the imagination and helpful generally on the subject of symbols, but be careful about taking any specific symbol interpretation too literally. When looking up a dream image you should regard the interpretation as valid for you only when you get a true tingle of recognition, and even then do not necessarily feel your search is complete.

It is often said that people in Jungian analysis dream Jungian dreams, people in Freudian analysis dream Freudian dreams, and so on. Witches will tend to dream 'witchy' dreams. If you dream of a cauldron, for instance, the dream may suggest a time of rebirth is at hand, or that you are about to become more creative (or pregnant!) or that a combination of things that are stirring around in your life at present is about to unify in a meaningful whole. You might wish to concentrate a ritual concerning this around your cauldron. For example, if you feel your life is fragmented perhaps you could write the names of the aspects you would like to bring together on scraps of paper, place them in the cauldron, light a candle to affirm the new life that will arise, greater than the sum of its parts, and then tie the pieces together with a cord of a colour you feel appropriate. Then put the bundle away in the back of your drawer.

I once had a dream concerned with a white horse – the sort that is etched in chalk on several hillsides in England. The dream in itself wasn't exactly scintillating, involving other, apparently trivial, elements. However, it stuck in my mind, and I felt I needed to visit this white horse. The white horse at Uffington in Oxfordshire, England is an ancient site. There I had a memorable and inspiring experience of Earth energies. There is insufficient space here to detail my visions,

but they can be experienced by anyone who seeks and loves the Earth, and I had them by literally following my dream.

Some dreams are 'big' dreams in that their imagery seems archetypal. Dreams of goddess or god figures, heroes, magical children, or any powerful symbol come into this category. You will know if your dream is archetypal by the sense of power and importance you feel. Such dreams can be relevant messages that something relating to the symbol is coming into consciousness, for instance, dreams of the Crone herald transformation. The Goddess may be inviting you to look inwards, reflect, harvest your Ideas, conserve your energy and explore the hidden and magical. Of course, images operate on many levels and this dream may also be a hint to develop a relationship with an ageing female relative.

Allow yourself to play with dream imagery when you have quiet moments. Don't have your nose stuck in a book for ages or feel you have to spend hours on your dreams or it will become far too time consuming. Do not crystallise your dream interpretation. We speak to our unconscious in simple symbols (e.g. circle, candle) but the unconscious speaks back in symphonies. Such images are meant to send us on quests, to ask what they mean, and this can be done in trancework. We explore this further in Chapter 9.

Do witches fly on broomsticks?

These stories probably originate from accounts of trances which feel like flying, somehow becoming linked to the broom, perhaps through sexual ecstasy. Brooms are fertility symbols – phallic handle in feminine brush – and were 'ridden' across the fields to encourage good crops. Also brooms are used for ritual and general cleansing – an innocuous possession for a medieval witch!

What are the chakras?

The chakras are a whole subject in themselves, explored in *Chakras for Beginners* in this series. They are energy centres, sometimes described as 'organs in the spiritual body' and awakening them is a process of spiritual enlightenment. They are usually regarded as being seven in number.

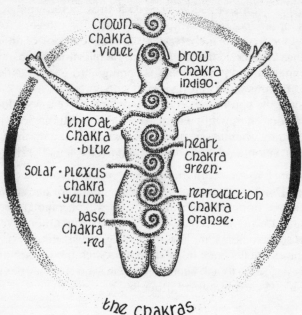

the chakras

The base chakra, at the bottom of the spine, rules the basic instincts and the adrenals. It is coloured red. The second chakra rules reproduction and intimacy. Coloured orange, it is in the lower abdomen. The third chakra is located behind the navel. Ruling willpower and life force, its colour is yellow. Fourth, the heart chakra, ruling love and compassion, is in the chest. Its colour is green. The fifth chakra is in the throat. Coloured blue, it rules creativity and communication. The sixth chakra, in the middle of the forehead, is coloured indigo and rules intuition, and the seventh, the crown chakra or 'many-petaled lotus' is coloured violet and rules enlightenment and mysticism.

Fully opening the chakras and raising the 'kundalini' or life force, coiled at the base of the spine is a matter of spiritual discipline and

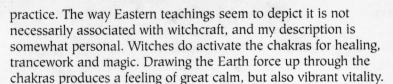
practice. The way Eastern teachings seem to depict it is not necessarily associated with witchcraft, and my description is somewhat personal. Witches do activate the chakras for healing, trancework and magic. Drawing the Earth force up through the chakras produces a feeling of great calm, but also vibrant vitality.

I found it took weeks of daily practice to learn how to open my chakras, but once accomplished it cannot be forgotten. It is best to start with the base chakra, and it is essential to be able to relax completely and utterly. You must ensure that you will not be disturbed, as anything that jars you once the chakras are open will be disorientating and may make you feel ill. Concentrate upon the base chakra, its position and colour, and imagine it glowing and growing. Continue relaxing and visualising, enjoying the sensation of being at peace – don't worry if nothing seems to happen, it may take repeated attempts.

As the first chakra opens you will feel a huge internal blossoming sensation, and you may feel flooded by the colour in question. Stay with this for a while; don't rush on to the next chakra until you have fully experienced everything and are sure the chakra is entirely open – this is a pleasurable sensation. Progress through the chakras one by one, from the base chakra, then the lower abdomen, and so on upwards to the crown chakra.

Once all the chakras are open, Earth energy – or whatever you wish to call it – can be drawn up through them. You will feel a surge of power and may twitch, as if with electric shock. Visualise the power as a stream of light, issuing from the crown chakra like a fountain and returning to the solar plexus chakra, so it is circulated like a battery. Now you are humming with power. This can be directed into healing or placed in the background while you proceed with your trancework. Close your chakras carefully after they have been opened, or you may feel ill. You may visualise them closing like lotus flowers, one by one, as rain falls upon them, or close them like eyes. Do this thoroughly, it is important for your well being. Eat or drink something to ensure they really are closed.

This is not a full set of instructions, so if you are interested please give the subject some in-depth attention. This is an important area. Seek and study for yourself, treat it with respect and it will yield you wisdom.

What is the Qabalah?

This ancient Hebrew mystical doctrine (also Cabala or Kabbala) is really more applicable to ritual magic, and some witchcraft traditions ignore it completely. However, many modern witches do draw upon it, and there may well have been cross-fertilisation between witches and magicians in days when persecution was rife. The basis of the Qabalah is the Tree of Life.

What is the Tree of Life?

Also called the Ets Chayyim, the Tree of Life is a kind of diagram of manifestation, starting with purest energy, descending to physical form.

The Tree of Life

It is composed of ten Sephiroth (singular Sephira) or spheres, and the twenty-two paths that interconnect them. Each Sephira represents a certain energy, or stage in the process of becoming or an aspect of being – so the Tree of Life is a kind of map of creation of the Universe, a blueprint of the process of any activity or situation, or a chart of the make-up of an individual. Each of the spheres is linked to a body in our solar system – Kether = Neptune, Tiphareth = Sun, Yesod = Moon, Malkuth = Earth, Binah = Saturn, Geburah = Mars, Hod = Mercury, Chokmah = Uranus, Chesed = Jupiter and Netzach = Venus. There is also Daath, the Hidden One, located below Kether and above Tiphareth, which is said to correspond to Pluto.

Allied to the Sephiroth is an extensive system of correspondences used in making spells – an idea we encountered in Chapter 2. The twenty-two interconnecting paths are each associated with a card in the major arcana of the tarot pack. As the Tree of Life is also a diagram of the human psyche, these paths can be travelled in a system of guided visualisation of trancework, called 'pathworking'. This is a way of inner exploration that can lead to revelations and far-reaching ideas, as well as shocks! However, many witches prefer simpler ways of travelling the inner worlds.

We must not leave the subject of the Tree of Life without noting something that is important to the philosophy of witchcraft, namely the Qabalistic saying that 'All the Sephiroth are equally holy'. Malkuth, at the foot of the Tree is equal to Kether, the Crown. Physical form is as valuable, meaningful and beautiful as the highest form of spirituality, for they are interdependent, and each is in a sense a form of the other.

WHY ARE SOME WITCHES CALLED 'WHITE WITCHES'?

This is to get away from the idea of black magic, and to sound respectable. Witches do not seek to harm people, but the term 'white' is a bit misleading, for witches are not saints and certainly make mistakes, however well-intentioned they may be.

What is a warlock?

This is not a term that is used by witches – male witches are called 'witches', too. 'Warlock' is a Scottish word meaning demon, wizzard or magician. It has come to be used for a male witch, but not among witches themselves.

Do witches believe in fairies?

They believe in Nature spirits, which are more or less the same thing, although different from the 'Disney' type of fairy. The faery folk are sometimes held to be the pre-Celtic peoples.

Do witches have familiars?

Having an affinity with animals, witches often keep pets and there may be a strong psychic bond linking them. Animals have also been used in divination, 'selecting' the appropriate symbol with a paw. Stories about familiars have been twisted and exaggerated.

Do witches shed blood in their rites?

Women are rarely fascinated by blood as they shed it monthly anyway. Menstrual blood can be a source of power, as can any blood. Of course, some people may shed blood, but it isn't really necessary. Anyone who does it **must** take proper hygiene precautions.

Is witchcraft passed down in the bloodline?

Yes, but no-one is compelled to be a witch because their parents are – it's a personal matter. There are growing numbers who have been drawn to the Craft by choice.

How do witches mark births, marriages and deaths?

Wiccan ceremonies for these occasions exist, and are generally based on ancient traditions. For babies the ritual is called a 'Wiccaning', for weddings a 'handfasting', and for funerals the term 'requiem' is used. Individual witches also have ceremonies for these transformation points, for they require some rite of passage to mark them. The three events are linked, and in many ways reverence for them is essential to witchcraft for they are at the centre of our existence and remain dredged in mystery – a mystery that is truly the essence of the Goddess and the God.

What is a handfasting?

This is a pagan wedding in which the couple jump the broomstick for fertility, and to mark the change that has taken place. Traditions vary with handfastings. Some say they last for a year and a day, after which they can be renewed or dissolved, as the couple wish. Others say nine years. The point is that this is not a 'till death us do part' vow, to be rigidly observed through degradation, misery and gross incompatibility. Witches make allowances for changes and mistakes, but this is not an invitation to laxity. Relationships need effort and staying power!

What is a Wiccaning?

This is the Wiccan equivalent of a 'christening' – a light and joyful ceremony, with the understanding that the child will be free to follow his or her own path, as an adult.

As witchcraft reclaims its inheritance and relevance to the community, pagan ceremonies for birth, marriage and death are being creatively developed by priestesses of an open style, who are available to preside (see 'House of The Goddess' at the back of this book). Alternatively, make up your own.

Are children allowed in the magic circle?

Occasionally they may be, as in a Wiccaning. However, the complex rituals necessary to effect a change in consciousness in adults are meaningless to a small child, who may well disturb the concentration of the adults. For older children the rituals might be bewildering or unsettling, and it is better that they be left out until they are adult and able to make up their own mind about the path they wish to follow. I don't put this forward as a rule that should never be broken, but the needs and nature of the child must always be the first consideration. Informal occasions and seasonal customs, however, are good for children's involvement. As witches we can learn a lot from a child's simple instinctual ways.

How does a witch family live?

Much like any other, really. When considering how a 'witch' family lives we are really talking about pagan families in general. They will be especially aware of the need to be as environment friendly as possible, and there is likely to be a tendency to choose natural fabrics and foods, to use essential oils rather than aerosols, to recycle cans, bottles and paper, and so on. Getting out into the countryside is especially favoured, and there will be a heightened awareness of the Earth and the passage of the seasons, and how these connect with what happens in our own lives. Pagan customs are evolving and borrowing from tradition, for example blessing the hearth and having a household shrine.

What festivals do witches celebrate?

Festival is intrinsic to witchcraft. Witches will tend to emphasise Yule, which is the Winter Solstice, two or three days before Christmas Day and be aware of the pagan symbolism of such things as the Easter

Egg, Father Christmas and the Christmas tree. The Spring Equinox, also called Eostar is perhaps the pagan equivalent of Easter.

The eight Sabbats or festivals celebrated by witches (see Chapter 7) can be marked by a party or special meal, which children may attend. Samhain, or Hallowe'en is especially important. This is an eerie time, when ghosts and spirits are felt to be abroad. It is important that children are encouraged to learn to cope with these things: to children they are a vivid reality. Children are far from reassured by being told that 'ghosts don't exist'. They believe that they do and they need to be able to incorporate this into the picture of a world that is 'okay'. If Mum and Dad deny darkness and mystery how can the child be anything but uneasy – even terrified? The monsters in children's fairy tales and such like are to help them come to terms with this and with their own destructive impulses that they need to recognise and accept before they can be in true control (as opposed to repressing them).

So, at Hallowe'en the pumpkin or turnip is hollowed out and a candle put in it, to frighten evil spirits and to create light as the darkness surges all around. Ghost stories are told and games like 'trick or treat' remind us all of the trickiness of the season, of life and of human nature – especially our own. To insist on an unalleviated diet of milk and prettiness is to invite the seeking of darkness in some much less healthy way. For darkness and death are parts of all of us.

Do witches wear different clothes, eat different foods?

Not really, although the 'natural' is likely to be favoured. Every witch is deeply aware that we should take only what we need and put back as much as possible.

I cannot imagine a present-day witch wearing the skin of any animal of endangered species. Some witches are vegetarian, feeling that is more respectful for life. However, even a cabbage has sentience, for bursts of static can be detected as its leaves are pulled off. Death is

part of life, so why not eat in accordance with it? Although animals have to be killed, they should be respected, and so game or free range, organically reared meat would seem to be the favoured choice. Some witches will eat only a type of animal they have killed themselves, at least once. Eating is one of the pleasures of life – it should be enjoyed!

Witches are mostly quite ordinary people, with normal jobs and often with families. Children are a precious sign of the renewal of life. They are treated with especial respect for their individuality. They are certainly never compelled to take part in anything against their will, or that they might not understand – in this witches are more careful with their children than many. Although brought up to respect the earth and pagan ways, they are not told what they 'must' believe.

PRACTICE

We have covered a lot of ground in this chapter and there are many things you can try. Why not start a dream diary? Or collect some ritual tools – your wand will be an important piece of equipment, so study the meanings of trees (see 'Further Reading') seek and choose. If you wish to practise with your chakras I would suggest more study. Start by reading *Chakras for Beginners* in this series. Perhaps you would like to try divination by tarot. Read *Tarot for Beginners* in this series. Take great care to select a tarot pack that appeals to you.

5 wiTches and sex

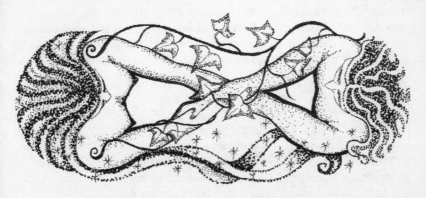

THE DAMNED THING of our education is that Christianity does not recognise and hallow sex. It looks askance at it, over its shoulder, oppressed as it is by reminiscences of hermits and Asiatic self-torturers.

Robert Louis Stevenson, *Letters IV*

What is the attitude of witches to sex?

There is something exciting and forbidden about both sex and witchcraft, although of course sex is now discussed freely. When the two subjects are put together, the imagination runs riot. The truth of the matter is that the sex life of most witches is much like anyone else's, although there is probably a difference in attitude.

Put simply, witches regard sex as sacred, and that is a general view among them. In many mythologies sex between the God and the Goddess created the Universe, and creates life anew each year in the seasons. Much that is creative can be seen as stemming from male/female polarity, whether it is the creation of a physical child or something more abstract, like a poem, in which the 'sexual' act is internal – a union with the 'inner man' or 'inner woman'. Creativity is sexy.

Sex is also sacred because it is enjoyable. It is a gift of the Goddess, who says 'Behold, all acts of love and pleasure are my rituals' (this is a quotation from a rite called 'Drawing Down the Moon'). Witches seek the divine through the body, not by transcending it, and sex can arguably be the most vivid expression of bodily joy. There are no dogmas to limit sexual expression. The only rule is 'harm none'.

When we make love we are in a sense enacting the union of the God and the Goddess, but that doesn't mean that homosexual love is less sacred. Sex is natural, but also special and powerful. Most witches will see that sex needs to be treated with respect, and people treated with consideration. It is certainly no part of witchcraft to abuse children, sexually or otherwise: nothing could be further from what all witches believe. This should be made crystal clear in the light of some stories that have been circulated.

Do witches get married?

They may well, if they have a committed relationship. It is a good basis for bringing up children.

Do witches have orgies?

This is another idea about witches that has its origin in fantasy. Few witches think an orgy to be reprehensible, but considerations like hygiene, infection and good taste need to be born in mind. In Neolithic times and the Dark Ages orgies may have been held as part of fertility rites, to ensure a good crop yield and an increase in

herds and flocks. Equally it is likely that stories of orgies were fed by an atmosphere of sexual repression. If you are sexually free the idea of an orgy becomes a bit boring. After all, why involve a crowd?

Group sex magic, a ritual in which several couples already in established partnerships, keep themselves to themselves in corners of a candlelit room, is a possibility. However, all these ideas are of marginal importance to witches, and they do not preoccupy themselves with them. Anyone who pursues witchcraft thinking is a passport to sexual licence and depravity will be sadly disappointed!

What does 'sky clad' mean?

This is a picturesque phrase for nudity. The human body is special, and so witches may choose to perform their rites naked. Nudity without shame is also a statement of freedom from prejudice, inhibition, coercion, and so on. However, some people do not like the idea of nudity, and that is equally acceptable. In any case, it may be cold and goose-pimples are not magical!

What is sex magic?

Sex magic takes several forms. One of the activities involved in making a spell is raising power. Sex is the strongest power source available. As an example, a couple who are both witches may direct the power of their orgasm into a spell – say for a home of their own – building up a clear picture of the house and releasing it at the strategic moment. This is simple in essence, but not always easy to do, for when you are involved in making love you may not wish to think about bricks and mortar at the transcendent moment. However, it can be fun practising!

Another type of sex magic involves the 'dreamtime' after orgasm. This can be a mystical interlude in which things are seen more holistically. Answers to questions may appear in the mind and what was obscure can become clear. You can learn to value and use this time as you become aware of its significance. Again, the trust between a committed couple helps and supports the process.

Tantra is another form of sex magic. Like many magical practices, Tantra raises personal power and awareness. There is also the achievement of states of ecstasy and union with the Divine. Tantra is an Eastern system and is not readily adapted for use by the Westerner. Plenty of literature is available on Tantra, and witches may practise it. The esoteric teachings of different countries bear recognisable similarities, and witchcraft and Tantra may have the same roots.

Many books are available on spiritual sexuality, and one is listed in 'Further Reading' at the back of this book. However, the idea that bodily ecstasy is sacred is a difficult concept for our culture. Tantra is not about anything gross or mindless but it is certainly explicitly sexual. There are many techniques but the highest goal is union with the Divine through the physicality of sex.

There is no doubt that Tantra needs to be approached seriously. Good intentions are not enough to protect the inexperienced from the ill-effects of meddling with the subtle energy currents of the body, and those who say Tantra should be learnt only at the hands of an experienced teacher are playing it safe. Comprehensive details about Tantra are, however, outside the scope of this book.

Finally, sex itself is magical. The mystery of the origin of a human life can never be completely explained, for all the advances in genetics. And the high achieved during sex is the best that most of us can hope to experience.

Is sex magic dangerous?

The dangers involved in sex magic are mostly emotional, and these should not be underestimated. When sex is used magically things can become intense. You may think you know what you are doing but this may turn out not to be the case. Things can emerge from the unconscious for which one is not – and cannot – be prepared. Someone could be badly hurt, or become disorientated or obsessed. At the least you may mess up a beautiful friendship. So sex magic is just for couples who are in love, committed, open with each other

and able to trust each other. If this is the case the use of magical sex will bring them closer together, but if not please be warned and steer clear.

Do witches use spells to attract a sexual partner?

Sexual love and fulfilment is what most of us want beyond anything else. 'Flags, flax, fodder and frig' are traditionally said among witches to be the requirements of a happy life. In our affluent society 'flags' (a dwelling) 'flax' (nice, warm clothes) and 'fodder' (good food) may be available to the majority of us. What does not always go smoothly, however, is 'frig' – finding someone we can love and enjoy sex with. Certainly witches do spells to attract love, but the important point is that it is love in general that is being attracted, not a specific person. You can visualise the kind of person you would like, but to attempt to influence a human being, except in exceptional circumstances, is just not on. That could infringe the freedom of all of us to choose our own path. From this it should be obvious that trying to pinch someone else's lover is not acceptable either – and spells to marry a favourite screen hero or heroine are also out – sorry! Sexual spells have a potent effect on the spellcaster, for the visualisation involved – and it needs to be graphic and concentrated to have any effect – is bound to inflame the passions. So sexy clothes and a brilliant smile are probably the best way to zap that special someone, and perhaps add some general attraction magic to give it all a bit of extra voltage.

What about celibacy?

I have not heard of this being practised by witches, but there could conceivably be magical rites where the prior observance of celibacy helped to increase power and concentration. To witches the body is sacred, and so transcendence is sought by means of it rather than 'rising above' – which could imply that spirit is holier than matter. However, in this, as all else, each witch is individual.

How about contraception?

Again most witches will follow mainstream opinion on this. However, it is advisable for each female witch to chart her menstrual cycle, noting differences in types of energy, dreams, feelings, etc. and to observe connections with the Moon's phases. Periods will often be found to have a direct relationship to the Moon, ovulation or menstruation tending to tie up with New or Full Moon. Exposure to the light of Full Moon has been known to stimulate ovulation. Observation of the Moon can help to regulate the cycle and the general benefits are enormous as a feeling of oneness and harmony with natural cycles grows. Graphs and thermometers are definitely not needed, for any woman who does this for a while will know precisely when she is ovulating and so can practise ways of lovemaking that can't result in pregnancy, if she so wishes. I feel sure the ancient 'wisewomen' knew all about this, and more. However, as they say 'Nature is a wonderful thing', and ovulation may be precisely the time you want intensely the kind of sex that *can* result in pregnancy.

How do witches feel about abortion?

There is no general rule. No dogmas attach to this subject and witches don't debate it particularly. There is a strong strand of feminism in witchcraft. Many witches will feel strongly that each woman has the right to determine how she uses her own body, and if she doesn't wish to play host to a new life then that is her choice.

Each woman in a sense has the power of life and death over her foetus. That is awesome, and some say fear of this power has been one of the drives behind patriarchy, to be controlled by Father-god and defined by rigid rules. Maybe even at the primitive foetal stage we are aware that our continuance depends to a large extent on the benevolence of our host mother. As the late astrologer Howard Sasportas put it, 'Some wombs are five star, others are two star – and some are shark-infested!'

Abortions are relatively easily come by now. Throughout history, during the Dark Ages, medieval times, and before, the combination of certain herbs, and simple ritual to cultivate the right state of mind would surely have been known and almost definitely have resulted in abortion. But abortion is no small matter. Each action we take changes us, and everything has a price. If you have become part of the current of creation by becoming pregnant, the decision to stop it is a big thing and you have to live with consequences later on that you may not imagine. In this sort of situation women need the support of other women, possibly those who have had similar experiences. This is not strictly about witchcraft, except that witchcraft is often allied to feminism and women's issues are seen by many witches as bound up in their beliefs and practices.

PRACTICE

You may like to give some thought to your sexuality. Is it sacred to you? Are there ways you would like to improve your attitude? Do you have inhibitions that trouble you? Do you feel the idea of sacred sexuality can help to enhance your life? How do you feel about contraception and abortion?

Female readers may wish to chart their periods by noticing if, and how, they tie up with the Moon by checking dates against the phases in your calendar or diary. Draw a circle and divide it into segments for each day of your average cycle, so it looks like a wheel with many spokes. Now you can allocate parts of each segment to physical matters, another to emotions, another to dreams (just note important symbols in brief, e.g. spider, sea) and anything that seems important. Draw some of the phases of the Moon around your circle to correspond with your cycle. Play with this idea, use coloured pencils to convey feelings, draw pictures around the edge. After you have done this for a few months you will get ideas of your own, so feel free to explore them. *Alchemy for Women* by Shuttle and Redgrove (Rider, 1995) is an excellent work to help with this.

6 THE PLACE FOR WITCHCRAFT

...when the moon is full
Ye shall assemble in some desert place
Or in a forest all together join.

from *The Vangelo*, translated by C G Leland

DO WITCHES MEET OUTDOORS OR INSIDE?

Outdoors would always, in theory, be the preferred place, as this is closest to Nature. However, most witches meet or do solitary workings indoors, because that way they aren't disturbed. Sinister stories are often heard about weird gatherings, but if any person or animal has been harmed true witches are not involved. There are some rituals which are open to anyone, held in parks for example,

sometimes for Earth healing or a similar purpose, and these are becoming more popular as witchcraft and paganism open up. Usually a witch will have a special place for rituals and spellwork indoors, and by constant use a strong atmosphere can be built up.

What is a magic circle?

This is a sacred space for rituals and spells. Creating the magic circle is an important first step, whatever one's working is to be about. We looked at the formation of a protective circle in Chapter 2 and this really is the same as the magic circle, but proper ritual strengthens it. The circle is in fact a sphere, surrounding the working area. It acts as a protective device, for in magical work stray energies can be harmful. The magic circle also concentrates the power, so that it isn't dissipated before the correct time. In addition, the circle is a halfway house between the everyday world and the world of spirit. We may experience things in the circle that do not happen elsewhere.

It is more convenient if the circle is actually marked on the floor. The space should first be cleansed. This can be done by imagining any negativity as grey clouds which you can sweep out of your circle by the motion of your hands. Banishing such as this is done 'widdershins' (anticlockwise). Positive actions are performed 'deosil' (clockwise), in the direction in which the Sun is seen to move in the northern hemisphere. Witches in the southern hemisphere often reverse these directions, for there the Sun is seen to move anticlockwise. The besom or broom is usually used to sweep out negativity. Salt and water are used to cleanse, by sprinkling. The circle should be drawn or 'cast' deosil starting in the north – again, reverse this in the southern hemisphere. You can use your finger, athame, wand, or whatever tool appeals to you. Visualise a stream of blue light coming from the tip of your finger, or tool, and forming the circle around you – clairvoyants are able to see this.

Once the circle is made it should not be broken, but if you must cross it open a doorway widdershins with your finger or magical tool, and close it deosil after you. Open and close again in the same way when you return. If you are in a Wiccan circle someone will do

this for you. Animals and children can usually pass through the circle without disturbing it, being naturally in tune.

It is usual to place candles at the East, South, and North points of the circle, and to have the altar at North, perhaps with several candles. It is also important to invoke the Guardian Elements at each of the quarters.

North is equated with Earth, East with Air, South with Fire and West with Water. Spirits of the North are called 'gnomes'. North is especially sacred because, in the northern hemisphere, it is the 'blind side' of the sky, home of all that is mysterious. The Sun and Moon are generally in the South. In the North are the circumpolar stars that never set. This is Caer Arianrhod, where souls of the dead retreat to heal and prepare for rebirth. (Arianrhod is Goddess of the Silver Wheel, of birth, initiation and rebirth.) North is associated with truth, groundedness and practical wisdom.

Air spirits are called sylphs. They are guardians of all that is swift, youthful and to do with the power of thinking. Their direction is East. South is the home of the fiery salamanders, of inspiration, energy and initiative, and in the West are the water spirits or undines. West is the direction of empathy, feeling and fathomless wisdom. Sometimes the West is associated with the Crone aspect of the Goddess, and sometimes this applies to the North. East is associated with the Goddess as Maiden. South is associated with the Mother.

A lone witch might ask the Elements to be present in words of her or his own. Turning first to North and holding high the arms the witch might say:

> Lady and Lord of the North
> Lend me your presence and your power.
> Give me protection, grounding and good sense,
> By hill and dale, deep cave, old bone,
> By fertile field and soil and stone,
> Be with me now, O Powers of Earth.

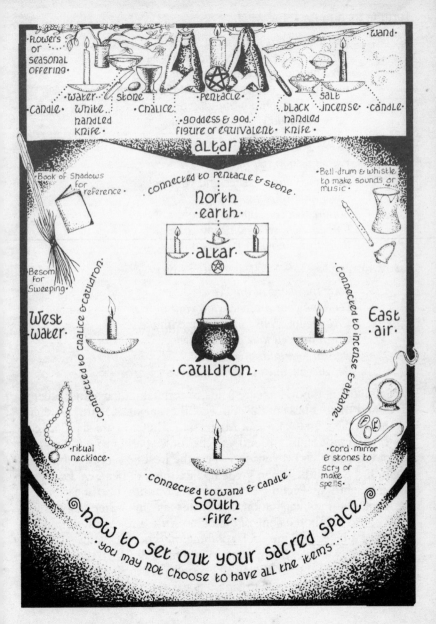

- flowers or seasonal offering
- wand
- candle
- water
- stone
- pentacle
- salt
- incense
- candle
- white handled knife
- chalice
- goddess & god figure or equivalent
- black handled knife

altar

- Book of Shadows for reference
- connected to pentacle & stone
- **North earth**
- Bell·drum & whistle to make sounds or music
- **altar**
- Besom for Sweeping
- connected to chalice & cauldron
- connected to incense & entrance
- **West water**
- **East air**
- **cauldron**
- ritual necklace
- cord·mirror & stones to scry or make spells
- connected to wand & candle
- **South fire**

how to set out your sacred space

·you may not choose to have all the items·

Turning then to East, the witch says:

> *Lady and Lord of the East,*
> *Lend me your presence and your power,*
> *Give me clarity, vision and swift thought*
> *By wind and cloud, tall mountain's height,*
> *By blue horizon, morning light,*
> *Be with me now, O Powers of Air.*

Then turning to South the witch says:

> *Lady and Lord of the South*
> *Lend me your presence and your power.*
> *Give me inspiration, energy and intuition,*
> *Bonfire, beacon, burning bright,*
> *Embers rich, wild lightning strike,*
> *Be with me now, O Powers of Fire.*

Lastly, turning towards West, the witch says:

> *Lady and Lord of the West*
> *Lend me your presence and your power.*
> *Give me love, wisdom and empathy,*
> *Green-hearted lake and river wide,*
> *Crystal fountain, ocean tide,*
> *Be with me now, O Powers of Water.*

While invoking Earth, imagine fields of corn, standing stones, silent caves and the richness of the soil, Feel the weight of Earth, its reality and rootedness. In the case of Air, imagine that you are standing on the top of a mountain. Around you the air is sparkling and blue, and a cool breeze blows on your face. Feel the freshness of Air, how bright and clear it is. When invoking Fire think of heat, wild dances, firelight, lightning. Feel the energy of Fire, warmth, heartiness and the leaping of the imagination. For Water imagine waterfalls, the swell of the ocean, the song of a mountain stream, the mysterious depths of a lake. Feel the cool, soothing presence of Water surrounding you like an embrace. When all is finished, thank the Guardians and bid them 'Farewell', starting at North and going deosil, and allow the circle to fade. Please note: you don't need a compass; you just need to be roughly in the right direction.

How should I ensure I have finished my ritual properly?

It is important to end spells and rituals thoroughly or you may feel oppressed or 'spaced out'. Consciously let go of energy by opening your palms, raising your arms and relaxing. Concentrate on your farewells to the Guardians – say to each of them 'merry meet' merry part and merry meet again' – imagine the doorway to their world closing. Take a few deep breaths, place your palms to the ground for a few moments, and eat a few mouthfuls of food. This will ensure a full return to the 'here and now'.

What is placed on a witch's altar?

A witch will probably like to honour each of the Elements upon the altar. Earth can be represented by a stone or pentacle, Air by the athame and incense, Fire with wand and candles and Water by the chalice and cauldron – the cauldron is often placed in the centre of the circle. In addition, statues or pictures of the Goddess and the God, special articles, necessities for spellwork, and of course any seasonal flowers or fruits, as an offering. The altar can be anything from a box covered by a cloth to something more elaborate.

What do witches wear?

Many witches like to work in the nude, for the subtle energies of the body are more free without cloth to restrict them. However, if nude working isn't suitable for some reason, you should try to have a special robe to wear only for working magic. It is easy to make such a robe – stitch together two rectangles of cloth on three sides, leaving openings for the head and arms. Choose a soft, natural fabric and make sure there is plenty of room for movement. You can tie the waist with a length of cord. A plain, dark colour is best. Keep your feet bare, if possible.

It is usual to have a special necklace to wear in the circle. The necklace can be of any natural stone that you feel in harmony with, or it could be a chain with an ankh, pentagram or other symbol on it – but it should be worn only when conducting rituals or working magic. Jet and amber are traditional favourites, and these are often considered magical mates representing receptive and projective forces respectively. Both have the property of becoming electrically charged when rubbed. Jet is protective. It is associated with Earth and the fifth 'element' which is spirit. Jet is fossilised wood millions of years old. Amber is fossilised resin of cone-bearing trees. It is associated with Fire and Spirit. Amber protects and banishes negativity. Some priestesses like to wear necklaces of alternating amber and jet.

Garters are also closely connected with witchcraft, often as a sign of rank. There is some reason for believing that the Order of the Garter – Britain's first chivalric order – has its origin in the Old Religion, namely witchcraft. The Plantagenets are believed to have been supporters of the Old Religion, and when Edward III was dancing with the Fair Maid of Kent (or the Countess of Salisbury) her garter fell down to the floor. Gallantly retrieving it the King said 'Honi soit qui mal y pense' ('Evil be to him who evil thinks'), but the implied challenge to the assembled company was 'Any of you lot want to make trouble over this?' The 'evil' in this case would have been the suggestion that there was any harm in witchcraft, for this lady's garter proclaimed her a witch. He then founded the said Order, with twelve knights for himself and twelve for his son, the 'Black Prince', making two groups of thirteen. Thirteen is a number often associated with witchcraft, linked perhaps to the Sun and the twelve signs of the zodiac. The founding of this Order conveyed the king's cryptic support for witchcraft and was an important gesture.

PRACTICE

You may like to set up an altar, if you have room – or set up a Goddess shrine, not necessarily where you intend to do rituals. On it place statues, symbols, offerings, or whatever feels right.

CHAPTER 7 how witches worship

...he to whom worshipping is a window, to open but also to shut, has not yet visited the house of his soul...

Kahlil Gibran, *The Prophet*.

how do witches worship Nature?

Just by being, by loving and taking part. Prescribed systems come from the logical part of the brain and so they tend to become rigid, and to ignore the transcendent – witchcraft is not like that. To love oneself is to love the Goddess. True love of self finds self in all life, and each witch is a priest or priestess. In worship of Nature witches traditionally celebrate the eight annual festivals or 'Sabbats'. The phases of the Moon are also observed, and Full Moon can be celebrated at an 'Esbat'.

Why are the seasons and the phases of the Moon important?

These are the rhythms we live by, and they reflect the patterns of human life. We can have a sense of meaning if we feel part of this universal rhythm.

What is the story of the seasons?

Like many things to do with witches, this is fluid. There are overlaps and paradoxes. Each individual witch can and should evolve his or her own picture from feelings and responses. In witches who are primarily Goddess-oriented the cycle may be celebrated in terms of the changing face of the Earth Mother alone (and some witches do not have eight Sabbats). For those of us who also think in terms of the God, the story goes something like this:

At **Midwinter** the God is born as son of the Goddess. She also can be seen as re-birthing Herself – bright baby, magical Maiden.

At **Imbolc**, the start of February, the Goddess is both Mother and Maiden. She has recently given birth and is fruitful and creative. She is also newly burgeoning along with the snowdrops and ewes' milk. She is Maiden. The God is young and growing.

At the **Spring Equinox** the God and Goddess are both youthful and vibrant with the excitement of Their potential.

At **Beltane**, the start of May, the God and Goddess, having come to maturity, mate and celebrate Their love with joy.

At **Midsummer** the Goddess is mature and glowing. The God changes. Slowly He begins to turn His face towards the realm of quiet and shadows. The Goddess is serene and fruitful mother to the glory of Nature.

At the end of August is **Lammas**. The Goddess as Earth Mother presides over the first harvests. In a sense the God now dies, cut down with the corn. In another sense He is reborn in all the provisions made from the harvest.

At the **Autumn Equinox** the Goddess is still gentle Mother Earth. This is really the second of the 'harvest' celebrations. The God is a shadowy presence.

At **Samhain**, the end of October, the God is true Lord of the Underworld. The Goddess is the Wise Crone. They are both old and clothed in mystery. This is a time of death, leading then to rebirth, once more at Yule/Midwinter.

We must remember that for witches in the southern hemisphere the wheel of the seasons is rotated through 180 degrees. For example, Australian witches who observe the 'where you are' approach, celebrate Samhain at the start of May, Midwinter on 21 June, etc, but not all witches choose to do this.

What are the Sabbats?

The word 'sabbat' is given various derivations, but the most appealing seems to be the French *s'ebattre*, which means to frolic. The Sabbats are an important part of the witches' tradition, and so we need to look at them at some length and to explore the meaning of each Sabbat. The Sabbats are also stages in the cyclic 'love story' of the Goddess and God.

the Wheel of the Year

There are Wiccan rituals for all Sabbats. I will give brief examples of the sort of thing a lone witch or 'hedge-witch' might do. These certainly aren't rigid – it is the underlying spirit that counts. You may need to recap on some of the terms used in earlier chapters.

The symbol that represents the Sabbats looks like the spokes of a wheel, for we are celebrating the round of the seasons, which is really a continuing spiral. There are four major Sabbats, which were the ancient Celtic fire festivals, and these are often viewed as times of 'high tide' of the seasonal energies. Ritual bonfires were lit at these times. The four lesser Sabbats mark the times when the tide turns. In general there is no better way to mark each Sabbat than by going out for a walk, looking, smelling, touching and breathing in the season.

The major Sabbats are Samhain/Hallowe'en, Imbolc/Candlemas, Beltane/May Eve, and Lammas/Lughnasadh. The lesser Sabbats are Yule/Midwinter Solstice, Spring Equinox/Eostar, Litha/Midsummer Solstice, and Autumn Equinox/Mabon. Witches are not literal about the dates, and in any case the solstices and equinoxes are determined by the exact position of the Sun, which varies slightly from year to year.

SAMHAIN – 31 OCTOBER

This is generally pronounced 'sa-*ween*'. It may seem odd to start with this festival, but Samhain was the old Celtic New Year and the start of winter, which in itself might seem strange. Why should this time of dying and ending be seen as 'new' year? This is the season of mists and mulch, rusty leaves, grey mist and an ever-increasing bite in the air. Life is fading, finding secret hiding places far beneath the hardening soil. The harvest is over, and now the unknown has to be faced in the coming winter. To our forefathers this was a crucial time. What should be bartered, and what kept? Which animals should be killed and which could survive the winter? And what of friends and loved ones? Old people and sickly children might not live to see the spring.

Autumn has often been described as poignant, but the Celts knew well that in facing endings we create beginnings. The most fragile phase of existence is often the initial one. And so at this time of dying we are aware that a new life trembles – somewhere – under the frost-brittle earth. We also know that when outer life decays, the inner life of the spirit is stronger. The Goddess is with us as Crone and Wisewoman. Her time of fruits and harvest is complete. Now She offers inward gifts of wisdom and magical power. Within Her glimmers the light of The Maiden, for She is also with us as Lady of Life-in-Death, and as Mother, too, for She carries the Sun God in the secrecy of Her womb. The God, having been cut down with the corn at Lammas, has made the journey into darkness and is with us as Lord of the Underworld.

The veil between this world and the spirit world is thin at this time, and it is traditional to ask the beloved dead to be with us – but they are asked, definitely never summoned. It is also traditional to scry or crystal gaze. Our theme at this time is 'Descent' – descent into our own Underworld, facing our fears, discovering our latent talents. We honour the God's descent by identifying with the way life is retreating, and by allowing what must die in our lives to do so. We honour the Crone by seeking Her wisdom. Of course, as witches we celebrate the preservation of life in seed and root, the gift of Knowledge.

Samhain Ritual

The circle is cast and cleansed and the Guardians are asked to be present, as usual. I like the candles on the altar to be black, and it is usual to have nuts, pine cones and apples also. Make sure you place a small bunch of dry, dead twigs there, too.

Stand at the centre of the circle, facing West, and begin to think deeply about the meaning of this time. Slowly say the following words, or something of your own:

> The Lord sailed slow into the West,
> The Lady waits and weaves;
> Time of Darkness, time of Death,
> Bald branch, bare earth, brown leaves.

Think about endings and retreat, and what it all means to you. Now think of all the things you really need to let go of, in order to make room for something else. When you are ready, say this:

> *He lets go, I too let go,*
> *Embrace the coming dark;*
> *I open palms and loosen grip*
> *On all that must depart.*

Open your palms and imagine all the unwanted matter dispersing like seeds upon the land – for that's what they are, seeds of some new potential that you can't yet see. Now put out all the candles except one on the altar. Sit in the centre of the circle and meditate. Call upon beloved ones who have died to keep you company if they wish. Scry, if you wish, perhaps by looking for images in a bowl of water that reflects the solitary candle flame. This is your 'underworld descent'. Take as much time over it as you like. Think also of the inner fires. This is a time of peace, when inspiration may unfold within you, new things become possible for the Earth.

You should have a cauldron, or bowl in the centre of the circle, with a candle in it. When you are ready take this candle to the altar candle and light it. (N.B. Although the other candles may be black, I would choose a white candle to stand in the cauldron.) Put the candle in the cauldron, sit and look at the flame and say something like:

> *In shadows deep we clearer see*
> *The light that flames within;*
> *In darkness whirling, stirring round,*
> *See, new life now begin.*

Watch the flame as it dances and glows. So does the life force, deep in the bark, under dead leaves, under stones... and it will awaken again. Consecrate some wine by drawing a pentagram over it with athame or wand – drink some and allow its warmth to make you feel more alive (or use fruit juice if you don't want alcohol). You need something to bring you out of the rather sombre, meditative phase. When you are ready, circle deosil around the cauldron, breaking into a dance if you like. With athame direct power into the candle that already flames there, feeling it surge with increased power. Then take up the candle and relight all the other candles. Vitality still pulses under the earth. Visualise the light of your inner sight gaining strength.

Take up the dead twigs. Name them after things that need to die, for yourself, for others, for the Earth. Affirm strongly that each twig embodies something undesirable that must go, for the good of all. Label the twigs if you like. Keep them and burn them later on a bonfire.

Cut an apple in half at right angles to the core, so exposing the little star shape at the centre. Save the pips to bury somewhere – they are the seeds of new life. Eat the apple in celebration, and drink wine in honour of the Goddess and God and the four Guardians. Do not forget to toast any of the dead you feel were present with you and thank them for being there. End your ritual as usual, by bidding farewell to the Guardians. It is especially appropriate to emphasise life in the teeth of the darkness by making love – either in the circle with your magical partner, if you have one, or later on.

YULE – 21 DECEMBER

Yule is the major turning point of the year, for now nights gradually become lighter and we are aware that the Sun is returning, although there are many cold days ahead of us. If we are lucky, frost sparkles and the long nights are crisp and spangled with stars. In Britain it is more likely that we have freezing rain and greyness, but it doesn't matter, because everywhere lights are bright and faces rosy in expectation of Christmas.

It is no accident that the birth of Christ is celebrated at this time, to coincide with the rebirth of the Sun. In the tradition of dying and resurrecting gods – of which there are many – the midwinter solstice seems the most appropriate time to celebrate the birth of the divine and magical child. The Church took over the symbolism of this festival, as with others. The commercialism of Christmas is often criticised, but really it is our instinct to affirm life when darkness is deepest. Also the glowing lights and baubles, as well as frightening away the shadows are a type of 'sympathetic magic' – if we make things bright enough down here then the Sun above will mirror our actions and return to shine on us. This still feels right to us, in spite of our literal modern minds.

The Goddess, as Mother, gives birth now to the God, with the shadow of His father/self protective in the background. In a sense, She also gives birth to Herself, for She too is renewed at this time. There is another way we think about the God now, for He has a light and a dark side (dark in this respect does not mean evil) called the Oak King and the Holly King respectively. The Oak King is king of the Waxing Year, from Yule to Midsummer. The Holly King reigns from Midsummer to Yule, as king of the Waning Year. So at Yule they battle and the Oak King wins – light is returning. Our theme at Yule is 'Rebirth'.

Yule Ritual

I like to have red and green candles, for these are Yule colours, of lifeblood and vegetation – but please note, white candles are always acceptable, so when in doubt or in the absence of others use them. On the altar place holly, mistletoe and ivy, and have a special large candle coloured red, orange or deep yellow as your Sun candle, securely fixed in the cauldron which is best placed in the south of your circle.

Cast your circle by the light of one altar candle. Then walk slowly around your circle. Say something like:

> The Sun retreated behind the mists.
> He descended to the Underworld and the Mother has mourned.
> All on Earth has been darkness and cold.
> Plants and animals have slept.
> We have withdrawn, to wait.

When you are ready, put out the solitary candle and squat near the cauldron, in almost the foetal position. Savour the darkness for a moment, the better to appreciate that it is coming to an end – the purpose here is not to envelop ourselves in darkness, as at Samhain, but to better affirm the rebirth of Light. Now strike a match and light your Sun candle. See, light is returning to the Earth. (N.B. You will need to be sure exactly where Sun candle and matches are so that you can find them in the dark. A bit of fumbling is a giggle, but if you really can't find the matches and you knock everything over, it could spoil your ritual.)

Unfold yourself slowly to a standing position and hold your arms wide and high, so you stretch joyfully. Say:

> Behold, the Mother has given birth to the bright Sun.
> Light returns to field and valley, mountain, lake and ocean.
> Shadows flee, joy returns.
> Blessed be the Great Goddess!

Move your cauldron with its lighted Sun candle to the centre, and with lilting movements, light all the other candles with a taper. Dance around the cauldron deosil, feeling the return of joy and life.

Go to each of the four quarters, starting in the North. Clap your hands and cry 'Wake up Earth, the Sun has returned', then do the same for Air, Fire and Water, visualising a rush of renewed energy for each of the Elements. Consecrate wine or fruit juice and celebrate the return of the Sun. Now sit quietly and watch the flame of your Sun candle. What is being reborn in you? Where are you now going to direct your energies? What are you going to 'shine' at? The Goddess and God will have a gift for you now. Allow pictures of what it may be to rise up in you. Thank them, and pledge a gift of your own to the Earth in the coming year. Make a final communion with wine or juice, and save some to pour out later upon the soil as an offering. Close the ritual when ready.

IMBOLC – 2 FEBRUARY

In northern climes the ground is still hard and the weather inclement at the start of February, but yet light is growing. In Britain, the first snowdrops peep out, the lambs are born and life tremulously stirs. It feels like the time to make new beginnings. This is a festival of light. The Goddess Brighid is thought of especially now, as patroness of poets and inspiration. We see the Goddess especially as Mother and Maid. She is Mother, having recently given birth to the Sun God. But She is also Maid – young and vivacious as the growing year. Imbolc is especially Feminine, and was a favourite time for initiation of priestesses. Our themes at this festival are 'Reawakening' and 'Initiation'.

Imbolc Ritual

After casting the circle as usual, consecrate nine small white candles. You may rub them with oils of frankincense, myrrh and sandalwood if you wish. Place these around your Goddess figure – stick them to a plate with Blu-Tack, if necessary. Light them slowly, deosil, saying: 'Light grows upon the land. Creativity flames within me. Blessed Be'.

From the final candle of the nine, light a large white candle to place in your cauldron. Sit in the centre of your circle, watch the flames and think about your creative projects. Dedicate one to the Goddess in the coming year. Take time to develop it in your imagination. Take three fairly thick strands of thread, preferably in natural fabric. All three may be white, or have one red, one white and one black for Mother, Maid and Crone, respectively. Knot the strands, anchor them and plait them slowly – or if you are good at macrame make something more complex. As you weave, let your mind dwell on your project – you are weaving your creative efforts for the year. When you have finished, make a final knot and release the spell by declaring your intentions in simple words and saying 'So mote it be'. Use your plaited strand as a bracelet, necklace or bookmark.

Go to the altar and reaffirm your dedication to the Goddess. Annoint yourself with lavender oil, or the three-oil combination above, diluted in almond or grapeseed oil (two drops per teaspoon) between the eyes, breasts and close to the genitals. Be careful, oils can burn sensitive tissues! Give yourself some time to meditate upon your renewed commitment. Commune with consecrated wine or juice and some cakes, and close your ritual when you are ready. (N.B. When we 'commune' we 'partake of the essence' – in the case of wine and cakes, these are gifts of the Goddess and God and we partake of Them when we eat and drink in worship and enjoyment.)

EOSTAR – 21 MARCH

At the end of March, spring is really on the way, despite the nip that lingers in the air. Primroses and cowslips are blossoming. Day and night are of equal length, but light is gaining. In the greenwood the young God is growing to manhood, and with Him grow the green

shoots and buds. The Goddess as Maiden delights in Her youth and beauty. Energy and promise are everywhere, but each of the equinoxes is a delicate time, of questioning and finding direction. Our theme is 'Resurgence' – we take a deep breath and decide where we will concentrate our efforts. An old story tells of the World Egg hatched by the Sun, and the egg is our symbol now. What are we going to 'hatch' in the coming summer?

Eostar ritual

I like to have candles that are bright green or yellow. It is often possible to buy spring wildflowers in pots, so have these upon your altar if you can (don't pick them from the wild) or put them in the South. Fill your cauldron with flowers, preferably still growing in pots, dance around the cauldron and visualise all the sparkling energy entering the blooms. Later you can put the flowers about your house, to herald light and new life coming into it.

Turn towards the South and welcome the Sun with upstretched arms. I like to ad-lib this festival, chattering about projects and growth, and imagining the rays of the Sun gaining triumphantly in strength. You could say:

> *At this time of growing light and warmth,*
> *I pledge myself to... and....*
> *Like the bright Sun pouring on to the land,*
> *I banish all that is negative.*
> *Hail to the power of the Sun,*
> *Growing strong to drive out darkness!*
> *Hail to the beauty of the Maiden*
> *As she dances on the green meadow!*
> *I welcome fresh new life into the land and into my life.*

You may like to sing *Lord of the Dance* for it is very appropriate at this time:

> *They cut me down but I leapt up high,*
> *I am the light that will never, never die.*
> *And I'll live in you if you'll live in me.*
> *I am the Lord of the Dance said He.*
> *Dance, dance, wherever you may be...*

You can also incorporate hen's eggs – free range – into your ritual, infusing them with power and painting them with food colouring to mark the plans they represent. Hard boil them first. Give them to friends and family to eat if you like, especially if the eggs refer to *their* plans. Dispose of the shells in a stream, or bury them in the garden later.

Close the ritual with consecrated wine or juice – orange juice is especially appropriate.

BELTANE – 30 APRIL

This is perhaps the most joyful of all the festivals. Eostar celebrated the fertility of Nature, but at Beltane we revel in human fertility. Beltane is flagrantly and gleefully sexual. The Goddess and the God have grown to maturity. He has wooed Her, She has taught Him the sensual mysteries and They mate in the greenwood in joyful abandon. Everywhere is bloom and greenery, warmth and sunlight are still growing and all things seem possible. Our theme is 'Fertilisation' – the sort of fertilisation that sets the seal on growth, as the conception of a baby should set the seal upon a relationship. This is a time to celebrate creativity, to revel in the pulse of the blood and the rising of the sap, and to join with the God and Goddess in the dance of love – but also to remember that the power of sexuality is not always used caringly. Witches may work magically for the healing of this. And we need to remember that the strong emotions sex gives rise to put us in touch with our own depths. So the Lady is with us as bright Maiden, glorious Mother, yet within Her beckons the Crone – and the way to inner knowledge can be hard and shadowy.

BELTANE RITUAL

It is traditional to decorate the altar with hawthorn. Place a large orange candle in the cauldron, with seasonal greenery and blossom arranged around it – the sexual symbolism of this is obvious! Skip or dance around the cauldron chanting:

> *Hail to the bright Sun returning,*
> *Rich and fertile passion burning,*
> *Wheel of Seasons, turning, turning,*
> *Hail Light and Life and Love returning.*

Light the candle saying something like:

> *The passion of the Goddess and God created land and sea,*
> *Moor and meadow, leaf, bud and root.*
> *Again they are recreated*
> *As the Sun lies warm upon the land.*
> *Hail to the Great Goddess!*
> *Hail to the Horned God!*

Annoint yourself, or your partner if you are working with one, upon feet, knees, genitals, breasts, lips and forehead. Or, if you are working with a partner, you may prefer to give what is called the 'five-fold kiss' in the same places, instead.

If you are a woman say:

> *By the grace and inspiration of the Maiden,*
> *Muse of the poets, free spirit, Lady of the Light,*
> *By the beauty and bounty of the Mother,*
> *Womb of creation, gentle Goddess, Lady of the Fire,*
> *By the wisdom and silence of the Crone,*
> *Keeper of the keys, stirrer of the cauldron, Lady of Magic,*
> *I celebrate my womanhood.*

If you are a man say:

> *By the power of the Lord of the Hunt, at one with his prey,*
> *By the joy of the Lord of the Dance, wild as the wind,*
> *By the branches of the great oak, strong to endure,*
> *I affirm my manhood.*

Consecrate some rose petals – dried petals will do – or leaves of mint and thyme. Take a moment to think of things in society and on Earth that need healing – perhaps rape especially. Put thoughts of that to one side. Hold out your hands or athame towards the petals and feel a stream of light coming from you into them. Imagine them

blossoming, growing – the fragrance and beauty fills the Earth, leaving no space for cruelty. Afterwards scatter the petals outside.

Consecrate wine/juice by tracing a pentagram in the liquid with your athame. Similarly, consecrate bread or cakes by inserting the tip of the athame. Say 'Great Mother, bless this food and drink for the joy of our bodies'. Make sure you have chosen something you find really delicious to celebrate with. Sit down and enjoy the food and contemplate the things you are bringing to fruition. If there seems to be nothing at present then visualise something you would like. Save some wine and cake and bury it in the garden later as an offering. Each Sabbat is best celebrated by making love – none more so than Beltane.

MIDSUMMER – 21 JUNE

This is the peak of the year, radiant with warmth and fulfilment – if we are lucky with the weather! The Sun hardly seems to set at all. Hanging baskets and flower beds are a riot of colour and the crops grow strong in the fields. In some ways we may see the Goddess has given birth to all this beauty. In others it is more apt to join with the Goddess and God in the heady delight of Their love. This is a time of consummation, but it is also a time of change. After orgasm comes the dreamtime, for fulfilment has sent us into another world, we see things differently with our inner sight. And fulfilment means change – not in the sense of anticlimax, for something we have truly wanted doesn't bring that. Yet it heralds new direction. In human terms requited love brings the responsibility of relationship, successful creativity means the need for a new goal. The God is changed in the ecstasy of union with the Goddess. Now light begins to wane and His strength turns inwards. As at Yule, the two sides of the God, the Oak King and the Holly King, battle, but now Holly wins. These light and dark faces are of equal value. Without death there is no life, without darkness no light. The Oak King can be seen as action and initiative; Holly King is the hidden and inward. This may be connected with our fears, but in embracing them we grow in power. We begin the journey into the meditative time of winter. Our theme now is 'Fulfilment and Change'.

Midsummer Ritual

Decorate the altar with summer flowers, place your cauldron in the South and sit behind it facing South. Have within it two candles, one dark green, one orange, and light the orange candle. Think of all the things in life that have brought you joy, and think of the changes you will make because of them. If this is a bad time for you, imagine how you would like things to be and visualise the good things you will do for yourself and others when these come about. Know deep within that this is a time of change. Say 'Farewell my Lord of Oak. Peaceful journey to the West. Guard the silent realms till we meet again.'

Light the dark green candle from the orange candle and snuff out the orange candle. Say 'Well met my Lord of Holly. Reign as darkness grows and guard the unfolding.' Move your green candle deosil into the West or North of your circle, for these quarters are both linked to darkness. Consecrate some orange juice, place it in your cauldron and dance around it, directing power into the juice. This is your parting offering for the Oak King. After your ritual, pour it out as a healing offering upon the earth. Consecrate some wine/juice and drink to the journey of the Oak King and your own future. Drink also to the brilliance of life that is everywhere at the moment. Close your ritual when you are ready, but move your green candle to a safe place, away from draughts, cats and children and let it burn itself out.

LAMMAS – 31 JULY

At the start of August everywhere is rich and gold. Butter-coloured fields are sandwiched between deep-green hedges. Earth is blessed with abundance, but the first touches of rust tinge the tree-tops and we begin to notice that the Sun sets earlier. I find Lammas the saddest of the festivals, although Nature's bounty is so obvious at this time. And yet all good things must come to an end, and there is a price to everything. This sounds morose, but facing it leads to greater strength, for the theme of this Sabbat is 'Sacrifice'. We see that the golden corn is stained by poppies, like drops of blood.

The Sun has poured his energy into the land and is now fading. With the yellow corn he is cut down, but then it is born again as the harvest fruits, vegetables, new-baked bread and all the other good things that are stored against the coming winter. There are many stories of dying and resurrecting gods that mirror this, and it seems that in earlier times men may have been sacrificed in honour of the dying God. Sometimes it was the King who was ritually slain, as appears to be the case with King Rufus. Rufus was an openly pagan English king who was killed in the New Forest at Lammas, 1100 CE, apparently at his own behest.

If ritual killing did take place it is certainly far removed from anything we would contemplate today. And yet the idea of sacrifice is significant. This is not the masochism that immolates the self, but it is a sacrifice for the sake of the self. In effect, it is a development of the Midsummer theme of change. Whatever we want in life we have to pay a price. Want a relationship? You will have to sacrifice independence. Want money? You will have to give up free time in order to work. It is a recognition that anything worthwhile involves putting something dear into it, and that can hurt, but it makes the goal more valuable.

In a sense, the Goddess gives birth now, to the harvest, and the God dies. In another sense, They are both still with us, generous and serene as we enjoy Their gifts – so this is a wake and a celebration.

Lammas ritual

Place first fruits upon the altar. I prefer honey-coloured candles now, if they are available. Have two ready-lit upon the altar, with a third, preferably bigger, in the middle. Wear a red scarf or cord around your waist. Face North, turn through East, face South and say:

> *Spread on the land the gold Sun lies,*
> *Sinks deep within, So sweetly dies.*

Turn West and say:

> *Now dear life spent and poppies red*
> *Stain the flaxen Sun God's bed.*

Turn to the North and your altar, saying:

> *So gather crops and brown bread rise;*
> *Now see fresh, new-born life arise.*

As you say the final line, light the large candle. Knot a piece of red cord so it forms a circle and pass this over the candle, circling the candle base. Think of all that is passing and of sacrifices you have made. Give them up freely as you pass the red cord over the candle, then look at the flame. You are transformed by your sacrifice as the flame transforms the wax. Something in you burns brighter as a result. Watch the flame and feel the inner fires of your spirit leap up.

Knot a second cord, this time in green, and pass that over the candle to lie on top of the red cord. These are the achievements that will be built on your sacrifice – your harvest. Think about your harvest and your hopes. Consecrate wine or juice and drink in honour of the Sun's power and your achievements. Have a small wholemeal loaf and some honey on a saucer upon the altar. Consecrate these by offering them to the four quarters, deosil, starting and finishing in the North. Hold them high and visualise the harvest riches entering this simple meal. Cut the bread and spread some honey upon it. Eat and drink communing with the season. Later share the bread and honey with friends and family, and scatter some on the land as an offering. Close the ritual.

AUTUMN EQUINOX – 23 SEPTEMBER

As at the Spring Equinox we are now poised upon a threshold. Light and dark are equal, but dark is gaining. Keats' 'season of mists and mellow fruitfulness' is upon us. The harvest is gathered and we begin to look forward to a cosy fire in the evenings, although days may still be warm. This is a crossover point. The balance is delicate and at times we feel it may tip over we could find ourselves in the world of Faerie.

The equinoxes have a subtle quality to them, felt especially in autumn – and drama may be supplied by stormy weather. The Goddess as Mother presides over stores of sharp-scented and juicy

preserves. The God is with Her as a shadowy presence, for this is the time when He begins His descent in earnest. Our themes now are 'Weighing and Sorting', so all may be in order for the coming winter.

Autumn Equinox Ritual

Blackberry-purple is a good colour for candles. It is traditional to place an ear of corn upon a plate on the altar. Cover this with a cloth. Place there also blackberries or other seasonal produce.

Stand in the centre of your circle and think about the meaning of the season. The Sun is fading. With it should go all unwanted habits, so what remains in the quiet time are the fruits of the harvest and the seeds of future life – you are sorting the wheat from the chaff. Have with you some dried leaves. Name them after anything you want to sweep out of your life, drop them deliberately on the floor and sweep them up. Keep them to scatter later into a stream.

Take the cloth off your ear of wheat, look at the wheat in silence, and then hold high the dish. Say something like:

The God has descended into the land
And now He makes His journey to the Underworld.
Days grow dim, nights grow long, but we who are wise do not weep,
For behold He has left behind His seed and His promise of return.
Blessed be the Great Mother, Blessed be the Harvest God.

Dance around your circle in celebration of the harvest and feel your cone of power rising in the centre. Direct it in healing to any part of the world where you know there to be famine. Commune with wine or juice and close your ritual.

What is an Esbat?

This is a Full Moon celebration – the time of the Mother, but She holds within Her the Maiden and the Crone. The Horned God is present, too, wild and wise.

To a witch Esbats are as important as Sabbats – they are the time for all magic (except banishing which is better when the Moon is waning). You may like to place a piece of quartz in your cauldron and dance around it, directing power into it for love or healing. You could scry. Perhaps you may like to make a herbal charm – a small bag containing Moon herbs such as lemon balm, sandalwood and jasmine oil – and use this to promote psychic awareness, peace and sleep. Full Moon is the best time to charge this with magical power.

At an Esbat we celebrate the silver light of intuition, all the enchantment of the Goddess as She reveals to us what we can never really communicate, by moonlight. As sparkling moondust quivers over field and tree and moonlight shadows speak of underworld knowledge, the pipes of the Horned God play for the inner ear – all the music of His love and sorcery. You may like to raise a willow wand to the Moon's silver face and chant:

> *Queen of shadows, Queen of light,*
> *Isis, Brighid, Lady bright,*
> *Hathor of the darksome night,*
> *Swell my magic power tonight.*
> *Queen of shadows, Queen of light,*
> *Waters sweep to tidal height,*
> *Witches' powers taking flight,*
> *Be present in my sacred rite*
> *Aradia, Diana, Levanah, Selene*

Dance, continuing the chant, raising power and directing it where you wish. I like to use a willow wand at Full Moon. You can catch Full Moon power by making nine knots in a red cord, the final knot joining both ends – you can use this for extra power when you do spells at other times. Drink a toast and sit quietly, eyes closed. If you have a drum, beat if softly – these are the footsteps of the goat-foot god, the dance of the Lady and Lord. See what thoughts and feelings come to you; you will be in a light trance – remember to write down your impressions afterwards. Close the ritual by eating and drinking, to ground yourself, and toast the 'Old Ones': 'Merry meet, merry part and merry meet again.'

PRACTICE

Mark Sabbats and Full Moons on your calendar or diary. Begin to think about the next one coming up and make notes of your impressions. What does this time of year mean to you?

Draw a large circle and divide it by eight lines so it forms a wheel. Label each section for a Sabbat, colour it and decorate it in any way you feel appropriate. This is your 'Wheel of the Year'. Put on it any feelings, colours or designs that appeal to you.

8 A WORLD OF WITCHCRAFT

Caelum, non animum mutant qui trans mare currunt
(Those who cross the seas change their homes but not their hearts)

Horace, *Epistles*

ARE THERE WITCHES ALL OVER THE WORLD?

Yes, but this book is concerned with practices that in general have their origin in European/Celtic tradition.

Do all witches do things differently?

There seem to be few major differences for witches of European extraction.

Are Australian or American witches different?

The short answer to this is not much. Most Australians and Americans are of European extraction, and the witchcraft we have been discussing is to a great extent Celtic and Anglo-Saxon. Before the Celts there were more ancient peoples, who departed the mainstream of life to live in forests and under hills. Some say these people, with their close bond with the Earth and the old gods, slid into another dimension and are still near us at times, as the Faerie folk. Others say their blood flows in the veins of witches. The basic beliefs of witchcraft are ancient, going back to the Stone Age, when society was probably matriarchal.

American witches

Old beliefs have always been present in the United States, as one would expect in isolated farming communities. The witchcraft trials in Salem, Massachusetts in 1692 are well documented. Twenty people were executed, but this was not a unique episode, so Americans have also had to cope with persecution. There is evidence to suggest that a witchcraft cult did indeed exist. Stories of Sabbats, naked rites to help crops grow, and magical signs painted on barn doors (notably among the Pennsylvania Dutch) all suggest that the Old Ways were followed to some degree. This is what one might expect in rural communities, for living close to Nature often gives rise instinctively to forms of witchcraft.

In many ways, the United States seems fresher and freer than Britain, but there seems to be more sensationalism and violence. Satanism and strange cults have linked sexuality with cruelty, and have been bracketed with witchcraft – although, of course, that is

not what witchcraft is about. The Charles Manson murders in 1969 were a notable example. So American witches have to struggle with the same sorts of prejudice as British witches. Broadly speaking, the Americans are more vocal than Britons are, and there are many American publications on witchcraft that are extremely useful. There are some very outspoken witches in the States, and many different forms of witchcraft. Of special importance is the strong feminist inclination. Some Dianic witches' covens do not admit men at all, and there is also a 'radical faerie' tradition of gay males.

The pagan scene in general is active in the United States, with a resurgence of Goddess-worship in all forms, and the word 'witch' may be used loosely to designate feminist pagans. Those who have access to the Internet will find many pagan and witchcraft sources, some of them really chatty and informative, with meeting places arranged and rituals created on-line, to someone's great expense!

AUSTRALIAN WITCHES

The picture in Australia is fairly similar to that in the United States. Rosaleen Norton, from the Bohemian quarter of Sydney is known as 'The Witch of King's Cross'. Rosaleen seems to have been an instinctual witch, born in New Zealand, who initiated herself as an adolescent and formed a coven who worshipped Pan and Hecate – among others, I am sure. Like any other witches these were Nature worshippers and had nothing to do with the devil. Rosaleen claimed that witchcraft had come to Australia with the immigrants from British rural areas.

There is a trend towards greater openness in Australia also, about which older pagans may be apprehensive, and yet it is important that witches and Goddess worshippers now feel they have to speak out (and are able to speak out). Australian witches and pagans are as varied as others, ranging from lesbian 'Wymyn's' Wicca to traditional paths. While pagans are diverse and independent, there seems to be a striking consistency among pagans worldwide. One of the pagan gods is Pan, and 'pan' means 'all'.

There are special problems for Australian witches, however, because they are in the southern hemisphere and many rituals are designed

for the northern hemisphere. And for a Nature-based religion this is important. For instance, in the North we place our altar in the North, for it is the dark part of the sky, home of mystery. The opposite is true in Australia and New Zealand. Likewise, the seasons are rotated. In the southern hemisphere Yule is at Midsummer in the North, Beltane comes at the time of Samhain in the North, and so on. Besides this, in the North the circle is cast deosil (clockwise) for that is the direction of the Sun's movement, but in the South the Sun moves anticlockwise.

There seems to be considerable debate among Australian witches about whether the old system is correct or whether a new system should be adapted, based on the southern hemisphere. Some witches are dogged traditionalists, others go with 'where you are'. Some alter the element/direction correlation so that North equates with Fire, West with Air, etc., but still place their altar in the North. The 'where you are' school rotate seasonal celebrations, so Yule falls at their midwinter in June. I have even heard that a unique version of the Wheel of the Year has been produced by someone, suggesting Australia has only three seasons. I think there is a great challenge for witches whose blood is largely European, but whose homes are in other continents. As witches we honour our ancestry, and we honour the land. Honouring both raises many issues if your origins in the recent past were elsewhere.

INDIGENOUS PEOPLES

Both Australia and America have indigenous peoples who have their own magical systems that are a basic part of their culture. In Australia, there seems to have been little cross-fertilisation with the Aborigines. Some indigenous people are willing to share knowledge with pagans, but I understand this is not common knowledge. The situation is similar with the American Indians. Americans have also been influenced by the beliefs that negro slaves brought to the continent. It is possible that a new shamanistic tradition could form, combining Celtic, American, Aboriginal, Polynesian and Melanesian influences – sounds exciting!

Americans and Australians especially need all their instincts and intuitions intact in order to develop meaningful systems and affirm their connection with the land – but today so do Europeans. For witchcraft, in the old sense has been all but eradicated and all witches have to form something new and relevant for our times. It is an interesting challenge for us.

PRACTICE

Think carefully about your own ancestry. Are you native to your part of the world, country, county, town? Do you feel at home there? How much do you know about your immediate environment? Try to find out as much as you can about local folklore, history and customs. And of course, do walk around your neighbourhood. That's part of being connected, and as we've seen 'connectedness' is a magical thing.

9 TAKING THINGS FURTHER

To find your own way is to follow your own bliss

Joseph Campbell

What should I do to become a witch?

Think carefully, for witchcraft isn't an easy path to follow. It is said 'once a witch, always a witch', and that can be taken to mean successive lifetimes, so that's quite an undertaking! However, in another sense there's not much point thinking deeply about it, at least not in the analytical sense. If you truly want to be a witch, then you are one, for it is something that comes from within. If you have doubts, then you aren't – at least not at this moment.

If you are curious, by all means find out as much as you can, but don't dabble with magic out of idle curiosity. It is too important for that. It's not that you will draw down something dreadful and sinister upon your head, although the experience could be scary; it is more likely that you will feel empty and depressed – the opposite to uplifted – for magic tends to yield up in the same manner in which it is approached.

If you wish to develop as a witch I am sure you will find your way. Study and practise – do not rush things. Take time to deepen your connections with the world around you – contact with Nature strengthens the magical self. When you are ready, prepare yourself with care and undergo a ceremony of initiation.

how will I know if this is the right path for me?

You will know. If it isn't right for you, you will continue to remain unsure, and you won't feel you are developing, so you will soon stop following the path. There is no need to agonise.

how can I meet other witches?

This is becoming easier as attitudes are becoming more open and witches themselves are speaking out to a greater extent. 'New Age' shops and alternative therapy centres usually advertise a selection of events taking place locally. Anything that concerns 'Women's Mysteries', 'Goddess Worship', 'Sacred Earth', and the like, may attract witches, or sometimes witches run the event. On the other hand, you may meet people who are close to the domain of witchcraft but can't bring themselves to use the word 'witch' because of all its connotations. If you talk to people and feel your way you will find out their opinions. One good way to meet other witches is through the Pagan Federation (see 'Useful Addresses'). You can ask to be put in touch with a regional co-ordinator, who can see that you meet like-minded people. But don't be too avid. It is said 'When the pupil is ready, the teacher will appear'.

how do I find a coven?

Again, the Pagan Federation is your best bet, or sometimes courses and lectures are organised by the High Priest or Priestess of a local coven. If you have decided that the coven way is for you, then you are choosing Wicca, as opposed to the way of the lone, or 'hedge' witch. Of course, this is not an irrevocable step, and many people progress from coven work to lone working, and vice versa. Covens are not sinister cults. You can leave whenever you want to.

The choice is not, however, restricted to Wicca. Different sorts of groups exist that do not follow this strict Wiccan path, but still use ritual and worship the Goddess, having a more community-orientated approach. In addition, you can always set up your own group if you know a few like-minded souls.

Witchcraft is not evangelical; groups do not tout for members, although most are eager to welcome sincere newcomers. Usually, the High Priest and Priestess will want to take time to get to know you, and vice versa. When looking for a coven, feeling comfortable is of the greatest importance. These are people with whom you will be involved with a fair degree of intimacy. Do not look for a 'powerful' personality, or be taken in by black garb, occult pendants and the like. Likewise, do not expect too much of your High Priest or Priestess. They won't necessarily be gurus. What they can do is teach you the Craft and give you the opportunity to develop, with some support. Leading a coven is a hard, and often rather thankless task! Look for reliability, sincerity and kindness, and return it!

Starhawk, in *The Spiral Dance* makes an important comment: 'In one sense, magic works on the principle that "it is so because I say it is so"... For my word to take on such force, I must be deeply and completely convinced that it is identified with truth as I know it. If I habitually lie to my lovers, steal from my boss... or simply renege on my promises, I cannot have that conviction.' It is worth bearing this in mind in one's own actions and when choosing ritual companions. Witches have a saying 'Perfect love and perfect trust' – this is the ideal.

How do I learn to meditate?

First, you need to learn to relax, and that isn't as easy as it sounds, for true conscious relaxation is something that has to be worked at in this hustle and bustle world.

You will need a routine. You should aim to devote ten minutes each day (not an hour once a week) to learning the art of relaxation. Select a time when you will be undisturbed and lie on your bed – for your subconscious mind will associate that with relaxing. Later, when you are proficient, you may wish to move on to a comfortable chair, for bed does suggest 'sleep'. If you are doing visualisation work you will need to stay awake.

Some people favour the method which tenses then relaxes each muscle in turn, starting at the toes and going all the way up the body, until reaching the many facial muscles and the top of the head. The action of tensing makes you more aware of each individual muscle, and so you are able to relax it thoroughly. Another method is to imagine that you are a candle with a gentle flame burning at the top of your head. All the soft, warm wax is running down over your body, taking away all tension with it – I prefer to use this method. Alternatively imagine all your muscles are powered by little men. Tell them to down tools and imagine them walking out – out of each muscle, down through your body and out of your toes, leaving you completely relaxed.

It doesn't matter which method you adopt, but take it slowly, giving yourself plenty of time to unwind, rechecking to make sure no tension has crept back, and so on. You do need to keep practising until you are reasonably sure that you are free of tension. This is therapeutic in itself.

When you are relaxed you can begin to visualise a 'sanctuary' in your mind – a special place where you can go when you need to be renewed, when you need to commune with yourself. Spend as much time as you need to construct this sanctuary, imagining all the details of it, until it is a reality to you. It truly is a reality on the astral plane. Make sure it is a place of safety and beauty, where you can feel at home: it could be a building, a woodland grotto, or

something that resembles a place in the material world that you love. It is best to invoke the Guardian Spirits of Earth, Fire, Air and Water at the four quarters, as you would for a magic circle, and affirm that they are present, guarding your special place.

You can go into your sanctuary whenever you feel depleted, confused or unsure, and rediscover peace. It is good practice to relax completely and enter your sanctuary for a while to meditate, before doing any form of guided visualisation, or before embarking on any ritual or magic. Practise entering your sanctuary and try to let your mind empty completely – but don't worry if you can't quite manage this. You have now achieved the ability to control your body and banish unwanted tension from it. Also you will have practised the art of visualisation and built something valuable for yourself on the astral plane. This will add to your inner confidence and feeling of personal power.

Guided visualisation

When you are in a relaxed state you may wish to go through a guided visualisation. You will need to record this on tape beforehand, or, if you are in a group someone will do the guiding. Below are examples of visualisation exercises that you may like to practise. (N.B. The power of the imagination is such that it doesn't matter what form your sanctuary takes – if an exercise calls for a path leading up from your sanctuary, you can imagine this even if your sanctuary is a boat in the middle of the ocean.)

Guided visualisations are also called trancework, and they are important to the witch. If you need the answer to something it can often be found by putting yourself into a trance – protective circle around you – entering your sanctuary and asking your inner guide. Ideas for rituals and all sorts of inspiration will come to you in this way.

Now relax completely and take a few deep breaths. You are ready to practise the guided visualisations that follow.

When you are ready to return to your sanctuary at the end of the guided visualisation, glide swiftly if you wish. Then come back slowly to everyday awareness. Take time to ground yourself – walk a little, place your palms on the floor, eat or drink something.

To find your inner guide

Enter your sanctuary. Allow the feelings of peace, tranquillity and safety to surround you. Know that you are about to embark on an important experience. Continue to feel completely relaxed and calm.

From your sanctuary a fight of shallow, wide, white steps leads up into a soft mist. Mist surrounds the steps on either side. You may not have noticed these stairs before. Whatever form you sanctuary takes, these steps lead up from it. Walk to the foot of the stairs. Do you want to go up them?

If the answer is 'yes', then start to climb the steps, slowly upwards, higher and higher, feeling a sense of deep peace and expectation. The mist above you is glowing softly. You may see special objects or artefacts on the steps – take note of these.

You realise you are getting to the top. Now the mist is becoming thinner. You hear faint music, like distant bells or wind chimes. As you climb higher you can hear the music more clearly. It seems to be all around you and inside you, soft and gentle. It is like a waterfall, a rushing stream, a cascade of temple bells, yet it is still gentle, soft and silvery.

You find yourself at the top and all the mist disappears. You are in a lush meadow. The sun is shining, the grass is emerald green – all the colours you see have extra depth and beauty. Look around you and notice plants, trees and animals. The music still surrounds you and you look ahead, where a glistening waterfall cascades over rocks and runs into a clear river.

Someone is coming towards you from the direction of the waterfall. You feel a sense of warmth and recognition. This is your guide. Greet her or him and listen attentively to anything she or he has to say. This is your friend, guardian and spiritual mentor. Ask her or him any questions you wish.

Now pause for ten minutes. Relax and make no attempt to control what unfolds. Let everything develop in its own way.

It is time to leave. Listen to your guide's final words. She or he may give you a gift or some special advice. This is something to treasure. You may wish also to give a gift – perhaps a pledge or merely a thank-you. Turn back into the mist and slowly go down the steps, carrying your gift back into your sanctuary, where you can place your gift for safe-keeping.

Now open your eyes and come back to everyday awareness. Be sure to write down what you have experienced. The guide that you met is your inner guide, a teacher who can help you with any issue that troubles you, from the most mundane to the most esoteric. Visit him or her frequently, so the relationship becomes deep and habitual – this is an important step on your spiritual path, and you will come to look forward to these encounters with a deep joy.

To explore dream symbols

Relax and enter your sanctuary. Within your sanctuary there is a soft robe of a colour you associate with safety. Brown is a good earth colour. Put on your robe. This robe will protect you on any journeys you take. When you are ready, step out of your sanctuary into a green field.

Take the time to examine the field. It is smooth and lush. Fragrant clover and daisies are scattered over the grass. Bees buzz, birds sing – this is a peaceful place. Now notice there is a path leading towards one corner of the field. Sit comfortably beside this path and ask your dream symbol to come to you along it. When it is in front of you ask it what its message is for you – you can ask, even if it is an inanimate object, for the answer will simply form in your mind.

(It is best not to invite dream imagery into your sanctuary. It can have all sorts of meanings and your sanctuary is your own safe and special place. If you do not obtain an answer you may get better results by approaching your inner guide, as in the first visualisation above.)

TO MEET THE ELEMENTAL SPIRITS

Step out of your sanctuary into the field you visualised above and follow the path as described to the corner of the field. Come out of the field through a wooden gate and follow the country path that lies beyond. Walk slowly, notice the trees, and hedgrows, feel the wind and the warmth of the Sun on your face. Take time to observe anything you see on your way. There are trees growing at either side of the path, branches touching gently above you.

On your left the ground rises, so you are walking beside a steep hill, that seems to be becoming more and more sheer. Overhead the branches tangle closer and the path beneath your feet becomes rougher and narrower. Rounding a corner you come upon a cave. Breathe deeply, inhaling the ancient smell of moss, damp and darkness. This cave leads to the heart of the Earth. Sit quietly beside it feeling conscious of the firm soil beneath your feet and the depth and deep peace of the cave. Ask the Earth spirits to come to you.

(If you record this exercise on tape leave five minutes' silence at this point.)

When your time with the Earth spirits is over, thank them and move on. Soon you come to where a great crystal waterfall plunges into an emerald lake. Sit near this waterfall, hold out your arms to it, hear the water splashing and lapping. Feel the tiny silver drops on your face. Breathe in the freshness, the purity. This is a place of great tranquillity and beauty. Look towards where the water cascades on to the smooth face of the lake and ask the Water spirits to come to you.

(Five minutes' pause again.)

When you are ready, thank the Water spirits for their company and move on. The trees part, the ground now rises and you have to climb steadily. The path becomes more rocky and the wind freshens. Higher, higher and higher you climb, until you find yourself at the top of a steep hill. Looking around you, you see miles and miles of undulating countryside, shimmering in a blue haze. There is a feeling of freedom and clarity. As the wind blows straight into your face, sweeping back your hair, open your arms towards it and ask the spirits of Air to come to you, borne on the breeze.

(Five minute's pause.)

Now move on, along the crest of this high ridge, towards the Sun. It is midday and the heat falls upon your face. In the distance you see a great glowing fire. The flames leap in a triangle of many colours. Come closer and closer to this fire. You feel comfortably warm and there is an air of tremendous vitality. All around the sparks are dancing, spangling the air and the rocks. Look deep into the red heart of this fire and ask the spirits of Fire to be with you.

(Pause for five minutes.)

When you are ready, glide back to your sanctuary. Remain there for a while, if you wish, to reflect on what you have experienced.

What form does initiation take?

This is an important ritual to mark inner change, a rite of passage to a new identity as a witch. Many lone witches prefer the term 'dedication' to 'initiation'. Dedicating one's life to the Goddess is serious as well as happy, and no less so when done in private as when in a group. It should be prepared for by Moons of contemplation.

Certain writers have said that initiation is not something to be undertaken alone, and that it needs the involvement of some form of priesthood to mediate the mysteries. But the path to divinity is open to us all and should not be controlled by any priesthood – Christian, Wiccan or whatever. Witches have always been individualists, and while there is much to recommend group study, anyone who wishes to follow a lone path should feel free to do so. We all have our own beacon to follow.

Any initiation ceremony, whether lone or by means of a group, has stages. The first stage is one of contemplation. If you have been thinking and studying for many months already then one Moon of this will do, but it should be the minimum. Start your lead-up period with a New Moon, and initiate yourself on the third day after the following New Moon. Meditate each day and study anything you feel led to: perhaps knowledge about different gods, healing or

whatever. If you are a newcomer than a year and a day, or thirteen Moons are good traditional timespans to devote to preparation. Please do not rush this.

It is usual to choose a 'witchname' which can be a name of a god or goddess (e.g. Epona, Celtic horse goddess) or a name from legend such as the Arthurian Gawain, to affirm new identity.

The ceremony needs to be preceded by purification, so take a leisurely bath with salt in it, or a few drops of lavender oil. Put on an old garment that you are prepared to shred or burn. Have a new robe ready, if you wish, and a little good quality oil – perhaps just pure vegetable oil, or use almond or grapeseed oil with essential oils frankincense, myrrh and sandalwood dissolved in the ratio two drops of essential oil to one teaspoon of carrier. Also have some wine to make a toast to your new identity, plus some cake or bread. Work nude if you can, but keep your garment with you, and some scissors.

Ensure that you will be alone for a considerable space of time – preferably the whole night following the initiation, and the entire day before. Before the ritual spend time outside, alone, preferably in some deserted place in the country. Begin your ritual after sundown. Assemble magical equipment and cast your circle as described earlier. Begin to burn incense. Allow a feeling of calm and transcendence to pass over you – this is an important moment.

You will have called upon the four Guardians in forming your circle. Turn again to North, hold high your arms and offer yourself to the powers of Earth, as witch and priestess. Do similarly to East, South and West in turn, then turn back to North (although if you are able to see the Moon in the sky, turn instead towards her).

Say something along the lines of: 'Great Goddess, bright Lady of the awakened soul, accept me .... (your 'witch-name') as your priest/ess. At this important hour of my life I dedicate myself in your name Isis, Aradia, Diana.'

Folding your hands over your chest and lowering your head, say: 'Horned One, God of the witches, give me your protection on my new path. Fill me with your energy and your joy Lugh, Herne, Cernunnos.'

(N.B. You can use any names of the Goddess and God that are evocative for you. This matters, mixed mythology doesn't.)

Take the oil and pass it through the incense smoke, through the candle flame (carefully!) and over your chalice or cauldron, and trace a pentagram over it with your athame, as described in Chapter 3. Annoint yourself between the eyes, upon the heart and the genitals, saying 'Let the mind be free,' 'Let the heart be free' and 'Let the body be free'.

Stand in the centre of your circle, face North and say: 'Great Gods, Old Ones, Powers of the Cosmos, accept me, ... (your witch-name), a true witch and pagan, as your priest/ess.'

Now sit yourself down comfortably, close your eyes and feel the powers of life accepting you. Feel your being expand. Still your mind and allow what pictures may come to surface in you. This is the most important part of your rite. Don't rush it. It is in this stillness, this inner cauldron, that you are refashioned as a witch.

When you are ready get up, hold your arms high and face North. Say: 'I, ... (your witch-name), witch and priest/ess embrace my new role with joy and celebration. My new life in the Goddess and the God begins here.'

Place wine in your chalice and trace a pentagram over it as you did with the oil. Drink wine and eat cake or bread in celebration of your union with the Powers of Life and the Goddess and God. When you feel ready you may like to dance in joy at your new state.

Take up your old garment and shred it with the scissors, imagining your old identity coming to an end with it. (If you have a fire to throw it in, so much the better.) Put on your new robe. Whenever you do magic or ritual in the future you will use this robe, or go naked.

Finally toast the Gods and the Guardians, saying 'Merry meet, merry part and merry meet again'. Thank the Guardians and bid them farewell. Allow your circle to fade.

Don't forget to record any dreams you have the following night!

The above is offered as an example. Consult other works and devise your own ritual as part of your preparation.

PRACTICE

This chapter has given you lots to do. It is important to practise your trancework if you wish to progress as a witch. However, it isn't really a good idea to do trancework every day as you may get 'spaced out' – the daily routine is only for learning to relax. Once you have mastered that, take your time with the rest. The exercises are best recorded on to a tape – leave pauses where I suggest and anywhere else you feel you would like them. If you don't like the sound of your voice, enlist the help of a soft-spoken friend to record the text for you.

If you intend to initiate yourself, read other sources of information first (see 'Further Reading').

AFTERWORD

Pounds the deep drum of the Mother
Pulsing belly, surging power
Bearing down into the warm earth
At the birthing of this new time

Carolyn Hillyer, 'Two Drumbeats' from the album *Heron Valley* and the book *Two Drumbeats*: *Songs of the Sacred Earth* (Seventh Wave Music, 1993)

What can witchcraft offer me in terms of personal development?

Witchcraft offers freedom, independence and personal power, which is power 'to' not power 'over'. The practice of magic and meditation leads to self-knowledge. It also offers a direct experience of the transcendent, if practised properly. If you want to be given laws and dogma, then look elsewhere for your path. In 'the Charge' the Goddess tells us '... Mine is the ecstasy of the spirit, and mine also is joy on earth; for my law is love unto all beings'. In the end what witchcraft can offer is a type of love, which is definitely not sentimental, but is part of a sense of oneness.

What can witchcraft offer society in general?

There is a political aspect to witchcraft – in a way there always has been – and that is growing. A strong feminist drive is inherent in Goddess worship and that extends to environmental matters. After all, Earth is our Mother, and instincts say do not foul your nest. The debate continues about how much harm we are doing to our environment, but it seems if we carry on in the same way the least we will do is make things uncomfortable for our species.

I know many people are fed-up with hearing about the environment. After all, you can't actually see the holes in the ozone layer. As for the vanishing rainforests of South America, few of us will go there.... If this is the way you feel, I do sympathise – at least in part. We've been told for so long that we can't have things. Now, just when life has never been so comfortable to most ordinary people, we're told we must stop driving our cars, or stop using so much fossil fuel. The majority of us want to be comfortable, and it's so easy to ignore what you can't see....

But if you're a witch you can see it. Not quite *all* the time, but most of the time. And it's bound to affect your actions. Awareness of the environment can sometimes seem a type of elitism, and at others the old hair shirt reincarnated. It shouldn't be either of these things. A basic love for the Earth can accomplish what self-denial never will, for one is a pleasure, the other a grind.

How can we reconnect with our instincts?

If you want to become more intuitive, get back to Nature. Go out in your garden, if you have one, and just 'be'. Really look at the growing things and the crawling things. Go out into park, wasteland, field and forest. Walk if you're energetic, sit if you're lazy. Camp if you don't mind the discomfort. Sit and look at landscapes. An old countryman said, 'Sometimes I sits and thinks, and sometimes I just

sits.' It's worth trying to just 'sit'; after all, that's a type of meditating. Let your hidden functions grow – don't force them. They are waiting to be invited out.

Of course, instinct is linked to femininity, and femininity has been devalued to such an extent that it is impossible to sort out. Like the roots of a willow, this attitude has entwined about and undermined the foundations of our society, and I think it will take many decades for us to be sure of all the implications. For instance, perhaps I am wrong. Perhaps femininity and instinct aren't so linked – perhaps they have both just been repressed simultaneously. Instinct is a male function too. There are many questions: the main thing is that we ask the right questions, like Parsifal in the myth of the Grail where the King and his land are sick. Parsifal needs to ask what the Grail is for – and the Grail is a most female symbol.

◄━━◆◆◆━━►

I would like to end with a question to you. If this book has been your first contact with the 'Old Religion' and the world of the witch, has it opened up your outlook, in some way?

I hope your answer is 'yes'.

fURThER REAdING

Aburrow, Yvonne, *The Enchanted Forest*, Capall Bann, 1993
Full of tree lore, this is a unique book.

Anand, Margo, *The Art of Sexual Ecstasy*, Aquarian, 1990
Tantric practices interpreted for the Western lover. Excellent bedtime
reading, but it won't get you to sleep!

Beth, Rae, *Hedge Witch*, Hale 1990
I treasure this book! Full of gentle wisdom and poetry, it really is a
must for a lone witch, especially a beginner, for the author manages
to frame into words everything that is important.

Brennan, J H, *Experimental Magic*, Aquarian, 1972
About magic rather than witchcraft, but it's clear and sensible.

Brooke, Elisabeth, *A Woman's Book of Shadows*, The Women's Press,
1993
Full of lore and information for the present-day witch.

Cunningham, Scott, *Wicca, A Guide for the Solitary Practitioner*,
Llewellyn, 1988
Lots of information for the lone practitioner. Scott Cunningham has
written many books that are a mine of information.

Farrar, Janet and Stewart, *Spells and How They Work*, Hale, 1990
A clear account of spellcraft generally. All books by the Farrars are
recommended.

Fortune, Dion, *The Mystical Qabalah*, Aquarian, 1987
Called the 'cornerstone of any decent occult library'. Those wanting
to study the Qabalah can't do better than to start here.

Green, Marian, *A Witch Alone*, Aquarian, 1991
Excellent step-by step introduction to lone witchcraft over thirteen
moons. All books by Marian Green are thoroughly recommended.

Rodway, Howard, *Tarot of the Old Path*, Urania Verlags, 1990 (Pack
and accompanying book)
Tarot pack compiled by witches, for witches. A beautiful set of cards
with designs that are meaningful to witches.

Serith, Ceisiwr, *The Pagan Family*, Llewellyn, 1994
Not about witchcraft, but invaluable for family traditions and
stimulating ideas.

Shan, *Circlework, A DIY Handbook for Working Ritual, Psychology
and Magic*, House of the Goddess, 1994
Breathtakingly practical and something of a personal testimony by
this dynamic priestess. Full of Mother wit. Thoroughly recommended.

Starhawk, *The Spiral Dance*, Harper & Row, 1979
Starhawk calls her book 'a toolchest for visionaries'. It is that, and
more. Essential reading.

Valiente, Doreen, *An ABC of Witchcraft, Past and Present*, Hale, 1973
Interesting overview and history of the Craft. All books by this
experienced witch and priestess are essential reading.

Worth, Valerie, *The Crone's Book of Words*, Llewellyn, 1971
Lots of spells, but they don't all follow the 'harm none' instruction.

USEFUL ADDRESSES

AUTHOR'S NOTE

The Pagan Federation (address on the next page) has asked me to make a few points about joining groups. Never, at any time, consent to anything that makes you uncomfortable, and steer clear of any individual or group that wants you to do that. No-one who has anything worthwhile to offer will expect you to do anything you find repellent. Nor will they seek to exploit you sexually. Occult 'advancement' can most certainly never be bought by trading sexual favours, and anyone who suggests it is highly suspect. On a few occasions young, keen and inexperienced seekers have been exploited. This is most likely (though, of course, not necessarily) to be by a self-styled male 'grand master'. This is not intended as a sexist remark, but it seems to have been the case in the past. Such occurrences are rare, but they can happen, as in other walks of life. If you are seeking a group, the PF can refer you to groups known to be ethical, and if you hear of a group you can write to the PF to ask if they know anything about them.

A few added words of my own:

I have stressed the importance of being alone with Nature but that, too, can be unsafe. So take a sympathetic friend along when going anywhere remote.

Witches are wild spirits. Ours is the song of the wind – and that is a freedom song. Remember that anyone who would deprive you of your freedom is depriving you of your witchdom. Listen for the voice of the Mother within you and follow it, whether within a group or alone.

N.B. When writing to any of the organisations below, please remember to enclose a stamped self-addressed envelope.

Church of All Worlds
P O Box 408
Woden ACT 2606
Australia
e mail: FTSWK@cc.newcastle.edu.au

House of the Goddess
A National Temple and Centre for Paganism
33 Oldridge Road
London
SW12 8PN
UK

Pagan Federation
B M Box 7097
London
WC1N 3XX
UK

Pan Pacific Pagan Alliance
P O Box 719
Castlemaine 3450
Australia

Wood & Water Magazine
77 Parliament Hill
London
NW3 2TH
UK
e-mail: dcohen@cix.compulink.co.uk

Please write to the author via The Publishers or E-mail:
100424.1723 @ COMPUSERVE.COM